THE WOMEN'S FINANCIAL CENTER
340 South 16th Street
Philadelphia, PA 19102

PLEASE SEND:

_____copies of The New Money Workbook For Women @ $8.00 each book plus $1.25 shipping charge for each copy. Pa. residents add 6% sales tax.

My check for $_____ is enclosed.

Make check payable to:

THE WOMEN'S FINANCIAL CENTER

MAIL TO: The Women's Financial Center
340 South 16th Street
Philadelphia, PA 19102

NAME_____

ADDRESS_____

CITY_____STATE_____ZIP CODE_____

Mailing address if different from purchaser

NAME_____

ADDRESS_____

CITY_____STATE_____ZIP CODE_____

The New Money Workbook for Women

The New Money Workbook for Women

A STEP-BY-STEP GUIDE TO MANAGING YOUR PERSONAL FINANCES

Carole Phillips

Brick House Publishing Company
Andover, Massachusetts

Copyright © 1988, 1982 by Carole Phillips
All Rights Reserved
No part of this book may be reproduced in any form
without the written permission of the publisher,
except for brief quotations if credit is given
to author and publisher.

Library of Congress Cataloging in Publication Data
Phillips, Carole, 1938-
The new money workbook for women.
1. Women—Finance, Personal. I. Title.
HG179.P457   1988   332.024'042   87-27657
ISBN 0-931790-82-4

To Andrew and Elizabeth

and all the women from whom
I've learned as much as I've taught

This is also the time and place to thank JoAnn Chadwick, Jane Nina and Kate Agostinelli for being research assistants *par excellence*; Michael Dickerman, Adelaide Ferguson, Helene Levine, Barbara Silver, Marcia Seifert and Harold Sampson for generously sharing professional expertise; and Dick Boylan, for teaching me the money business.

Contents

1 **How Much Am I Worth?**
An Introduction to Financial Planning   1

    The Five Steps of Financial Planning   1
    STEP 1   GETTING ORGANIZED   2
    A Guide to the Personal Income Statement   3
    A Guide to the Personal Financial Inventory   5
    STEP 2   SETTING GOALS   10
    My Financial Goals   11

2 **How and Where to Hold Your Nest Egg**   12
    How Much Should You Keep in Your Nest Egg?   12
    The Married Woman's Nest Egg   13
    Where Should You Keep Your Nest Egg?   14
    Deposit Insurance   16
    Where Should You Keep Transaction Balances?   17

3 **Whether a Borrower You Should Be**   19
    How Much Can You Afford to Borrow?   19
    Where to Borrow   20
    Special-Purpose Borrowing   22
    Credit Life Insurance   23
    Before You Apply for a Loan or Credit   23
    If Your Application is Rejected   24
    How to Check Your Credit Record   25
    Why a Married Woman Should Have A Credit Record in Her Own Name   26
    To Establish Your Credit Rating   27

4 **Nobody Knows What's Coming Tomorrow:**
Life, Disability and Health Insurance   28
    Guide to Calculating Your Life-Insurance Needs   30
    What Kind of Life Insurance Should You Buy?   32
    When is a Dividend Not a Dividend?   34
    Naming the Players: Owners and Beneficiaries   35

Payment of Life Insurance Proceeds   35
How To Apply for Payment of a Life-Insurance Policy   36
Disability Insurance   37
How is Disability Defined?   38
When Should Disability Payments Begin and How Long
    Should They Last?   38
How Much Disability Income Do You Need?   38
What Kind of Health Insurance Do You Need?   39
What Kind of Health Insurance Do You Have?   40

5   Taking Stock of Stocks and Bonds   42

Why Buy Stocks and Bonds?   42
The Risk-Return Trade-Off   43
Choosing Stocks for Different Financial Goals   44
How To Pick A Stock   44
The Effect of Inflationary Expectations on the Purchase
    of Growth and Income Stocks   45
Five Ways to Become A Stockholder   45
How to Read The Stock-Market Page   47
Bonds   49
How to Read a Bond Certificate   49
How To Read The Bond-Market Page   51
Why Interest Rates and Bond Prices Change
    (and One Goes Up When The Other Comes Down)   51
Who Issues Bonds?   52
Types of Bonds   54
Registered and Bearer Bonds   54
How To Compare Taxable With Tax-Free Yields   55
Choosing a High-Quality Bond   55
Where to Buy Stocks and Bonds   56
Should You Hold Your Own Securities?   57

6   The Feeling is Mutual   58

Why Buy Mutual Funds?   58
Load and No-Load Funds   59
Open-End and Closed-End Funds   60
Different Funds for Different Objectives   60
How to Pick a Mutual Fund   63

How to Buy a Mutual Fund   64
How to Keep Up With Your Mutual Fund   64
How to Sell Shares in a Mutual Fund   65

7   There's No Place Like Home   66
How to Buy a House   67
Where to Go for a Mortgage   68
Kinds of Home Financing   69
Should You Refinance Your Existing Mortgage?   71
Secondary Financing   72

8   Real-Life Monopoly: The Real Estate Investment Game   73
Why Buy Real Estate?   74
Choosing a Location for a Real-Estate Investment   75
Things to Think About Before You Buy   75
If You Lack the Means or Experience to Do It Yourself   78

9   All That Glitters: Silver and Gold   79
You Should Buy Silver or Gold Only If   80
How to Buy Silver and Gold   80
Where to Buy Silver and Gold   82

10   Delectable Collectibles   83
When You Buy Collectibles   84
Do Not Purchase Collectibles Blindly Through The Mail   84
What Are Your Collectibles Worth?   85
When You Sell Collectibles   86
Tax Tips for Collectibles Investors   86

11   A Tax Shelter Is Not a Home   88
How Limited Partnerships Work   89
Should You Dispose of Your Tax Shelter?   90
Is There a Good Post-1987 Tax Shelter?   91

12 How to Enjoy Life After a Working Life   93

What You Can Expect to Receive From Social Security   94
What You Should Know About Your Employer's
    Retirement Benefits   94
Distribution Options and Tax Consequences
    of Employee Retirement Benefits   96
How Much Will You Need to Retire?   96
Individual Retirement Accounts (IRAs)   100
Keogh Plans   102
Salary Reduction Plans   104
Simplified Employee Pension Plans   105
IRA Rollovers   105
Annuities   105
How Much May Be Contributed to an Annuity?   107
Annuity Payment Options   107
How Much Will It Cost to Buy or Sell an Annuity?   108
Accumulation Table   109
Compound Interest Table   110

13 Estate Planning: Who Gets What After You're Gone   112

Why Everyone Should Have a Will   112
What Are The Duties of An Executor?   113
Who to Name as Executor   115
Executor Fees   115
Estate, Gift and Inheritance Taxes   116
Annual Tax-Free Gifts   116
The Use of Trusts in Estate Planning   117
How Trusts Work   118
What Assets Will The Trust Receive?   119
Whom to Name as Trustee   119
Where Things Are   120

14 Who Owns What: His, Hers and Ours   121

The Different Kinds of Legal Ownership   121
Why Every Married Woman Should Have Assets
    in Her Own Name   122

Prenuptial Agreements   123
Divorce and Separation Agreements   124
Living Together Agreements   124
Income and Estate Taxes   125

15 The Tax Man Cometh   126

Keeping Up With Changes in The Tax Laws   126
Consult Experts   126
Keep Good Records   127
Who Must File a Tax Return?   128
Which Tax Form Should You Use?   128
How to Calculate Your Taxable Income on Form 1040   129
Estimating the Coming Year's Taxes   135
Will Your Tax Return Be Audited?   136
What to Do if You Are Called for an Audit   137
Tax Tables, 1987 and 1988   138

16 Nobody Looks Out for You as Well as You Do: Financial Planning in Action   140

STEP 3 DEVELOPING A FINANCIAL PLAN   140
How Much Must You Save and Invest Each Year?   141
How Much Must You Set Aside Each Year?   142
Where Will The Money Come From?   142
STEP 4 IMPLEMENTING YOUR FINANCIAL PLAN   143
Where Do You Go For Help?   143
How To Choose A Financial Advisor   143
STEP 5 PERIODICALLY REVIEW AND REVISE YOUR PLAN   146

Preface

The first edition of **The Money Workbook for Women** was written for the many women who were interested in becoming good money managers but didn't know where to begin. The reaction from readers has given me the most gratifying experience in my professional life. Thousands of women in the U.S. and Canada—even in places as far flung as The Bahamas and Guam—used **The Money Workbook for Women** as a quick and easy resource for everything ranging from applying for a first mortgage to opening an IRA.

This new edition is just as committed as the first to guiding the novice money manager through unfamiliar territory in language she understands. It also is an opportunity to eliminate outdated material and include recent changes that have taken place in our tax laws and in the financial marketplace.

The format of **The Money Workbook** was developed from The Money Work*shop* for Women I taught in the late seventies and early eighties at Temple University's Division of Educational Services for Women and Men. Rather than talk about investments, insurance and other financial decisions as if they were unrelated, my course considered each topic within the framework of an individual's total financial needs. This gave the material a unifying concept—the concept of financial planning—to provide week-to-week continuity and tie together the bits and pieces of personal money management.

The Temple course was a do-it-yourself workshop, with the accent on *work*. Assignments were structured so that students had to apply class discussions to their own financial situations. During the first session everyone had to figure out a savings program that was appropriate for her own means and needs. At another session each student was asked to look at her family's insurance coverage and decide if more, less or a different kind of coverage was needed. In other words, my students learned by the most effective learning technique there is: by doing.

The Money Workbook is based on the same principle as the workshop. The first chapter presents an introduction to financial planning. The next fourteen chapters take you through the seven categories of personal financial decisions—saving, borrowing, insurance, investing, retirement planning, estate planning and tax planning—but always in the context of *your* particular needs and objectives. When you arrive at the last chapter,

Financial Planning in Action, you will be prepared to choose financial instruments and to select professional advisors to help you achieve your objectives.

I am often asked, "Why a 'Money Workbook for *Women?*' Don't men need this information as much as women do?" The answer is: Yes and No. There are few male counterparts to the divorced or widowed homemaker who must make do for the rest of her life on investments from the sale of her house or a modest insurance settlement. There are few men whose wives meet with lawyers and accountants to make plans about which the husbands have slight knowledge or interest. And I have yet to meet a young male professional with a good job and money in the bank who rejects the idea of buying a house because it destines him to be single for the rest of his life!

A book written by a woman and titled **The New Money Workbook for Women** is intended to send the same sort of signal as the "Automotive Repairs for Women" course offered by a women's service organization in my community. It says, "This is for those of you who never wanted to know or thought you were incapable of learning how this business works. Now you need to know. We specialize in beginners." It also says, "There's no obligation on your part to master all the intricacies of high finance (or repair other people's cars). It's okay if you just learn enough to become better informed about your family's financial situation and feel comfortable asking questions when you have to talk to your stockbroker or accountant (or mechanic)."

Despite rumors to the contrary, men are not born with and women are not born lacking a gene labeled "good money manager." No one is born knowing this stuff; we all had to acquire it by reading, asking questions and getting hands-on experience. I'm a woman and I've done it. So can you!

>Carole Phillips
>Barnegat Light, New Jersey
>September 1987

1 How Much Am I Worth? An Introduction to Financial Planning

Financial planning means making a comprehensive evaluation of your current financial situation, setting realistic goals for the future, and determining how to reach those goals.

Financial planning is the most effective way to organize your financial life. It provides a structure within which you can think ahead, set goals, and coordinate the financial decisions that allow you to reach your goals.

The Five Steps of Financial Planning

Step 1: Getting organized.
Step 2: Setting goals.
Step 3: Developing a financial plan (**How much** you need and **when**).
Step 4: Implementing the plan (Choosing **investments** and **advisors**).
Step 5: Periodically reviewing and revising your plan.

Why plan?

For peace of mind and financial security.

What can happen if you don't plan?

Listen to Joan, an unemployed office supervisor:

> When I was working, I spent every penny I earned and more. I spent it on clothes, my apartment, vacations, you name it. If it had a price tag, I bought it. I had a good job with the city, but because of budget cutbacks, my department was closed. So there I was with a couple of

hundred dollars in the bank, and a lot of bills to pay. I owe $2,000 on my car and about $3,000 between the credit card and other bills. At first, it didn't bother me. I assumed I'd get another job. But it's been two months since I've worked, and now I'm scared. I can't sleep nights. When I go out for a job interview, I'm so tense and desperate, I know I make a terrible impression. And all I think about is how I wish I'd put away some money while I was making it.

Ruth, a 60-year-old widow:

When my husband was alive, he took care of me. I thought he would always take care of me. When he died, I discovered there was nothing left. He had borrowed on his insurance policy, and what Social Security gives you is not exactly what you would call extravagant. I still don't know where the money went. All I know is that I had to give up my house. I had to go out to work. I wasn't trained to do anything. Let me tell you, standing on your feet in a store all day is no picnic.

And Sheila, a 43-year-old homemaker:

I worry about our future. My husband is a lawyer and I know he makes a good living, but I don't know if we're doing the right thing with our investments. It's difficult to get him to sit down and talk about it. Sometimes we do nothing at all. The money just sits in the bank. Then Paul decides we've got to invest it, so he calls his stockbroker and we buy some stock. Sometimes we've done well, other times we've gotten badly burned. It's hard to know what to do. You get so much conflicting advice. One person says you should have a lot of insurance, another person says he doesn't believe in insurance. How do you know what to do? How do you know who to trust?

STEP 1
GETTING ORGANIZED

If Joan or Ruth or Sheila came to my office for counseling, the first thing I would ask her to do is fill in the Personal Income Statement and the Personal Financial Inventory shown on the following pages. This is an important part of the first step in the process of **getting organized**.

You should not buy one share of stock, one life-insurance policy or any other financial asset until you have a clear picture of where you are and where you want to go.

A Guide to the Personal Income Statement

The Personal Income Statement helps you see where your money comes from, where it goes, and how much you have left over to save or invest. Prepare the income statement for a full calendar year. Last year's income tax return, your checkbook stubs and bank statements should be helpful. If you expect this year's income or expenses to differ significantly from last year, estimate the items that will be affected.

PERSONAL INCOME STATEMENT

Income List all sources of income, even those on which you pay no taxes, such as Social Security or child support (alimony is taxable!). "Taxable" interest is earned on such savings instruments and investments as savings certificates, money market accounts, U.S. Treasury securities and corporate bonds. "Nontaxable" interest is earned on municipal bonds. It is exempt from federal income tax—and from state income tax if you live in the state of issue.

If you are married and have income of your own, you might want to list your income and expenditures separately from your husband's.

Wages and salaries	_____	Trust income	_____
Commissions	_____	Alimony	_____
Tips	_____	Child support	_____
Bonus/Profit-sharing	_____	Social Security	_____
Dividends	_____	Pension	_____
Taxable interest	_____	Other (specify):	_____
Nontaxable interest	_____		_____
Rental income	_____		_____

TOTAL SOURCES OF INCOME _____

HOW MUCH AM I WORTH?

Expenses List personal and household expenditures according to whether you incur the expense monthly, quarterly or annually. Transfer totals for each expenditure to the right-hand column.

Total income less total expenses is, or should be, your surplus for saving or investing. If the difference is negative, it means you spend more than you earn. You can't plan for the future without the money to plan with. Examine your income and expense items. What can you do to increase income or cut back on spending this year?

(Use appropriate column)	MONTH	QUARTER	YEAR
Mortgage or Rent			
Utilities			
Telephone			
On-going household			
Home maintenance and repairs			
Home decorating			
Clothing			
Personal care			
Medical and dental			
Insurance premiums you pay			
Life			
Disability			
Homeowner's or Tenant's			
Medical			
Automobile			
Car maintenance and gas			
Public transportation			
Recreation			
Entertainment			

Travel   _____   _____   _____
Tuition   _____   _____   _____

Nonmortgage interest   _____   _____   _____

Gifts   _____   _____   _____
Contributions   _____   _____   _____
Membership dues   _____   _____   _____

U.S. income taxes   _____   _____   _____
State income taxes   _____   _____   _____
Local taxes   _____   _____   _____

Other (specify):

_____   _____   _____   _____
_____   _____   _____   _____
_____   _____   _____   _____

TOTAL ANNUAL EXPENSES   _____

SURPLUS FOR SAVING AND INVESTING   _____

A Guide to the Personal Financial Inventory

The Personal Financial Inventory is like the balance sheet a business prepares to get a picture of its financial situation for a current period.

Assets are listed separately from liabilities. Assets are everything you own. *Liabilities* are your debts or obligations to others. The difference between what you own and what you owe is your *net worth*, or what you are worth on the day you fill in the inventory.

Don't be concerned if some of the assets and liabilities listed are unfamiliar to you. They will be explained later in the workbook. Also, if you are not certain what category an asset or liability belongs in, write it down as "other." The important thing is to get it all in.

HOW MUCH AM I WORTH?

PERSONAL FINANCIAL INVENTORY

An **asset** is any financial or material possession that has monetary value. A savings account is an asset. So is the furniture in your home. In financial planning, we classify assets as *liquid, marketable, nonmarketable* or *personal*.

Liquid assets are cash or assets which can be converted to cash quickly and easily, such as a checking account or savings account. A liquid asset has the same, or close to the same, value it had when you acquired it, plus interest earned in the interim. Liquid assets are *marketable*. They can be sold outright (e.g., savings bonds) or funds can be withdrawn as needed, such as from a bank money-market account or money-market fund. Some life-insurance policies have a *cash* value which may be borrowed from the insurance company or for which the policy can be sold back to the insurance company. The cash value, listed on a chart in a policy contract, depends on the age of the policy.

OWNED BY:	Self	Spouse	Joint
Checking accounts	_____	_____	_____
Savings accounts	_____	_____	_____
Money-market accounts	_____	_____	_____
Credit-union share accounts	_____	_____	_____
Savings certificates	_____	_____	_____
U.S. savings bonds	_____	_____	_____
U.S. treasury bills	_____	_____	_____
Money-market funds	_____	_____	_____
Cash value of life insurance	_____	_____	_____
Other (specify):			
_____	_____	_____	_____
_____	_____	_____	_____
_____	_____	_____	_____
TOTAL LIQUID ASSETS	_____	_____	_____

Other marketable assets are financial resources like stocks, bonds and real estate that also can be sold but at a price which might be more or less than you paid for them. Assets in this category usually are investments that you hold onto longer than you do liquid assets.

If you own stocks, bonds or mutual funds, ask a broker for their current value or look up the prices in the business section of your newspaper. Only real estate purchased as an investment should be listed as a marketable asset. Personal residences are nonmarketable assets.

OWNED BY:	Self	Spouse	Joint
Common stocks	_____	_____	_____
Preferred stocks	_____	_____	_____
Mutual funds	_____	_____	_____
U.S. notes and bonds	_____	_____	_____
Corporate notes and bonds	_____	_____	_____
Municipal bonds	_____	_____	_____
Real estate	_____	_____	_____
Gold and silver	_____	_____	_____
Collections (art, etc.)	_____	_____	_____
Other (specify):			
_____	_____	_____	_____
_____	_____	_____	_____
_____	_____	_____	_____
TOTAL OTHER MARKETABLE ASSETS	_____	_____	_____

Nonmarketable assets are assets that have monetary value to the owner but cannot be sold, like your interest in a company pension fund, or can be sold only through private negotiation, such as the sale of a business or professional practice.

Primary residences and vacation homes are included among nonmarketable assets because the dwellings we occupy are purchased primarily for comfort and convenience and not as an investment.

OWNED BY:	Self	Spouse	Joint
Vested-interest pension plan	_____	_____	_____
Profit-sharing plan	_____	_____	_____
401(k)	_____	_____	_____
Indiv. Retirement Account	_____	_____	_____
Keogh plan	_____	_____	_____
Stock options	_____	_____	_____
Business interest	_____	_____	_____
Nonmarketable securities	_____	_____	_____
Annuities	_____	_____	_____
Tax shelters	_____	_____	_____
Primary residence	_____	_____	_____
Vacation home	_____	_____	_____
Notes receivable	_____	_____	_____
Other (specify):			
_____	_____	_____	_____
_____	_____	_____	_____
_____	_____	_____	_____

TOTAL
NONMARKETABLE ASSETS_____   _____   _____

Personal assets are possessions like cars, books and jewelry which are purchased for personal use. They are included in the Personal Financial Inventory to complete the picture of your total wealth.

OWNED BY:	Self	Spouse	Joint
Household goods	_____	_____	_____
Automobile	_____	_____	_____
Jewelry and furs	_____	_____	_____
Other (specify):			
_____	_____	_____	_____
_____	_____	_____	_____
_____	_____	_____	_____

TOTAL PERSONAL ASSETS_____   _____   _____

Total assets The sum of your liquid assets, other marketable assets, nonmarketable assets and personal assets is the current value of your **total assets**.

TOTAL ASSETS   _____   _____   _____

Liabilities A liability is a debt. It is any financial obligation owed to another individual or to an institutional lender. A loan from a relative or a loan from a bank is a liability. So is your home mortgage.

List the *total* amounts you owe *currently* on your credit cards, retail charge accounts and other household or personal bills even if you repay on an installment basis. Since the purpose of the Personal Financial Inventory is to give you an accurate picture of your current financial situation, you want to know what you'd be left with if all your debts were paid off tomorrow.

Taxes past due are literally that: unpaid tax bills, such as federal income taxes you did not pay on April 15. All recurring taxes appear as expense items on your **Personal Income Statement**.

OWED BY:	Self	Spouse	Joint
Retail charge accounts	_____	_____	_____
Bank credit cards	_____	_____	_____
Household and personal bills	_____	_____	_____
Loans	_____	_____	_____
Mortgage (principal home)	_____	_____	_____
Mortgage (vacation home)	_____	_____	_____
Second mortgage(s)	_____	_____	_____
Home-equity loan	_____	_____	_____
Security-margin loan	_____	_____	_____
Taxes past due	_____	_____	_____
Other (specify):			
_____	_____	_____	_____
_____	_____	_____	_____

Total liabilities Add up your liabilities.

TOTAL LIABILITIES   _____   _____   _____

Net worth Deduct **total liabilities** from **total assets** to determine your **net worth**, what you are worth today.

NET WORTH = TOTAL ASSETS − TOTAL LIABILITIES

Getting organized is the first step in the financial planning process because we must know where we are today before we can say where we want to go tomorrow.

Where do *you* want to go?

STEP 2
SETTING GOALS

Before you begin to save and invest, you should know *why* you want financial assets and *how* you intend to use them. Prudent financial planning suggests that having a safe and liquid "nest egg" and adequate insurance coverage should be everyone's top priorities. After that, you're on your own.

Do you want to supplement current income? Be financially independent? Are you concerned about retirement? Taxes? Inflation? Do you want to plan for your children's education or start your own business? Do you have a handicapped child or dependent parent whose security must be provided for?

Think about it. Write it down so you can *see* what you say you want. You can write down anything, so long as it's realistic for your financial situation. And list your goals in order of their importance to you. If you can't have or do everything you want, you can try to provide for the things you want most.

Married women: Ask your husband to prepare a list of his financial goals. You will learn a great deal about one another's priorities when you compare his list with yours.

My Financial Goals

1. A safe and liquid nest egg
2. Adequate insurance coverage
3. _____
4. _____
5. _____
6. _____
7. _____
8. _____
9. _____
10. _____

2 How and Where to Hold Your Nest Egg

Everyone should have a safe and accessible nest egg for emergencies. We call this "rainy day" money.

Think of your nest egg as a kind of insurance, the most certain and immediate source of financial security you can depend on. It's your buffer to live on between jobs, the way to pay a plumber who insists on cash when the pipes burst, the money you always know will be there if you need it.

The money in your nest egg must be *safe* and *liquid*. Safety means there is little or no risk of loss. Liquidity means having access to cash as soon as you need it. You want to earn the highest *interest* (also referred to as *return* or *yield*) you can on savings, but yield is secondary to safety and liquidity.

Safe and liquid interest-earning savings instruments are listed on pages 14-16. (They also appear as "liquid assets" on the Personal Financial Inventory on page 6.) You can use these same savings instruments for other financial goals, but the reverse is not true. The more risky non-liquid investments you might consider for such long-term goals as retirement are not always suitable for a savings nest egg.

How Much Should You Keep in Your Nest Egg?

One-quarter of your annual income after taxes is often suggested as a reasonable amount to set aside. Under this guideline, if your after-tax income were $25,000, your target figure would be $6,250. Your need to save more or less than one quarter of your after-tax income depends on your age, whether you own other assets, the stability or uncertainty of your job situation and whether others are financially dependent on you.

The amount you keep in your nest egg is a *target* figure, not an amount you must save each year. If you must draw upon your nest egg in an emergency, build it up again as soon as possible.

Calculate Your Savings Goal

		Example
My(our) after-tax income for 19__	$_____	$25,000
	x 1/4 =	x 1/4 =
My (our) accumulated savings should be	$_____	$ 6,250

The Married Woman's Nest Egg

Sandy and Laura have joint checking accounts with their husbands, but they also have savings accounts of their own. This is *their* money to do with as they please.

Sandy, a high school English teacher, has a deposit made from her paycheck to her share account in the teachers' credit union every payday. Laura, a homemaker, makes a deposit out of her household money at the savings bank next to the supermarket before she does her weekly food shopping every Friday.

If Sandy and Laura save $10 a week for 52 weeks, at the end of a year they will have $520 plus interest. If they can save $20 each week, they will have $1,040 plus interest. $1,000 earning 5.5% in a savings account will be worth more than $1,300 in five years. If Sandy and Laura put $1,000 into their accounts every year for five years, they will have almost $6,000.

This is the least they can earn. As you'll learn later on in this workbook there are higher yielding investments that can make money grow faster for the long-term goals you have, like going back to college or starting a business.

Whether you work in a factory, a store, an office or at home, it's easy to get started on a savings program of your own. Just take "The Saver's Pledge."

The Saver's Pledge

I promise to save $ _____ per week each week until _____ , 19___ , at which time I shall have $_____ .

                                            Signed,

                                            (your name)

Where Should You Keep Your Nest Egg?

The savings instruments you should consider are listed below. The savings instruments you *choose* are the ones that suit *your* preferences and needs.

Carol and Mike have four children, and barely make it from paycheck to paycheck. They inherited $5,000, used $2,000 to pay some bills, and bought a $3,000 insured savings certificate. Being "locked in" for six months removes the temptation to spend if the money were kept in a more accessible money-market fund. It also gives them the flexibility to reinvest at a higher yield if interest rates are higher when the certificate matures.

Lucy and Alec, on the other hand, have a joint income of $75,000 and a combined net worth of $200,000. They use a tax-free money-market fund because they are in a high tax bracket. It provides a higher yield to them than the comparable after-tax return on all other equally safe and liquid short-term savings vehicles.

And then there is Alice. She retired recently from a well-paying job as senior buyer for a major Chicago department store. She transferred her savings from a tax-free money-market fund to a taxable money-market fund because she now is in a lower tax bracket and will keep more of the higher pre-tax yield.

Everyone's needs are different.

Passbook savings accounts Savings accounts for which deposits, withdrawals and interest are recorded by the depository institution each time a transaction is made. A passbook account is liquid and safe but has the lowest yield among savings options.

Statement savings accounts Savings accounts for which the account holder keeps her own record of deposits, withdrawals and interest. Receipts and quarterly statements are provided by the depository institution as confirmations of transactions. Some statement savings accounts pay higher rates than passbook accounts.

Savings accounts are available at commercial banks, savings banks, and savings & loan associations (S&Ls). Savings banks and S&Ls are sometimes referred to collectively as *savings* or *thrift institutions*.

Credit union share accounts Savings accounts in a credit union, available only to credit union members. Credit unions often pay higher rates than banks and S&Ls, but funds must be kept in an account for one month or more to earn interest.

Money-market accounts Savings accounts that might require the maintenance of a minimum balance (for example $1,000). Money-market accounts pay higher rates of interest than traditional savings accounts.

Savings certificates Contractual agreements that a saver will keep a specific amount of money in a depository institution for a specified period of time (three months to ten years) and receive a specified rate of interest. Certificates pay higher rates of interest than regular savings accounts. Some interest, and perhaps a part of the principal, is lost if a certificate is redeemed before its maturity date. Interest earned on savings certificates may be reinvested or paid to you on a monthly or quarterly basis.

Not all certificate issuers pay the same rates, so it may be worth taking the time to shop around. However, if one certificate issuer is paying much higher rates than all others, be certain before you buy that it is a well-managed, well-capitalized institution that is aggressively seeking new deposits and not a poorly managed, under-capitalized outfit with a high risk of failing.

Savings certificates are available at commercial banks, savings institutions, credit unions and stock brokerage firms.

U.S. Treasury bills Issued by the U.S. Treasury for three, six and twelve month periods for a minimum of $10,000 with $5,000 increments. Treasury bills are safe and relatively liquid, but if you need to sell one before it matures, it may be worth less (or more) than you paid for it. "T-bills" can be purchased from a regional Federal Reserve Bank (at no extra charge), depository institutions and brokerage firms (with a service charge).

Savings bonds The smallest denominated bonds issued by the U.S. government. Series EE Bonds are sold for a minimum of $25 with a $50 redemption value. Series HH Bonds are sold for a minimum of $500 with a ten-year maturity. They are "liquid" in the sense that both may be cashed in without penalty six months after their issue date. On the other hand, no interest is earned by Series EE Bonds held less than a year or Series HH Bonds held less than six months. The stated interest rate on Series EE Bonds is paid only on bonds held five or more years. A lower yield in the form of a lower redemption value is paid on Series EE Bonds cashed in prior to maturity.

Series E Bonds that reached final maturity after 40 years no longer earn interest. If bonds are redeemed for cash, taxes will be due on the deferred interest. Taxes will continue to be deferred if matured Series E Bonds are exchanged for Series HH Bonds.

Money-market funds Mutual funds which purchases large-denomination money-market instruments, such as Treasury bills and bank-issued certificates of deposit. The interest earned, which might be higher than the rates paid on savings accounts, is passed along to the shareholders. Money-market fund interest rates change as the yields on the securities in their portfolios change. The minimum investment is as low as $1 to $500. There is no sales charge for putting money into or taking money out of your account. Share prices remain the same at all times. There is no minimum holding period. Money market funds are safe, but not as safe as insured savings instruments. They are liquid and relatively high yielding for short-term investments.

Tax-free money-market funds Made up of investments that earn interest exempt from federal and some state income taxes. The formula on page 55 can tell you if your tax bracket warrants tax-free income. Money-market funds may be purchased directly from a fund's sponsor or through a stockbroker.

Terms and rates on savings instruments change frequently, and new savings vehicles are being introduced all the time. Check things out with your depository institution or stockbroker before you buy.

Deposit Insurance

Accounts and savings certificates of $100,000 or less issued by all federally chartered banks, S&Ls and credit unions and by most state-chartered banks, S&Ls and credit unions are insured for the full amount of your account. Some money-market funds are covered by private insurance. "Insured" means that if a depository institution fails and is unable or unwilling to give you your money, you will be reimbursed by its insuring agency.

Where Should You Keep Transaction Balances?

Transaction balances are what we used to call checking accounts; that is, the money you use to pay bills or other financial obligations. Now that you can earn interest directly on transaction balances, or transfer money instantly from an interest-paying savings account to a non-interest-earning checking account, all your money can be working for you all the time. Transaction accounts are offered by depository institutions and some mutual fund organizations and brokerage firms.

NOW and Super-NOW accounts NOW is an acronym for Negotiable Order of Withdrawal, or a checking account that earns interest (a Super-NOW earns more interest). Depository institutions either require that a minimum balance be kept at all times in NOW accounts, charge for each transaction and/or charge a monthly maintenance fee.

Money-market accounts A money-market account may be used as a checking account if you don't use too many checks. Each month you are permitted to withdraw money from your account by writing three checks *or* through six "pre-authorized transfers" (This means you authorized the bank to pay your mortgage, telephone bill, insurance premium, etc., each month). In addition, you may make unlimited withdrawals from cash machines or from live tellers.

Credit union share drafts Checks that credit union members may write against their interest-earning share accounts.

Automatic teller machines (ATMs) Through the use of a plastic card and a secret identification number, you can withdraw funds from your interest-earning NOW account, share account or money-market account. You also may transfer funds from an interest-earning savings account to a non-interest-earning checking account in the same or different depository institution. ATMs usually are open twenty-four hours a day, seven days a week. If your card issuer belongs to a national ATM network, you can have access to your interest-earning cash out of town.

Telephone bill-paying accounts A depository institution is provided with a list of creditors you pay frequently; e.g., the mortgage or rent, utility bills, insurance premiums, department stores, etc. You continue to receive bills from the creditors. When payment is due, you telephone the depository institution and authorize payments from your account of a specific amount to each creditor's checking account in the same or another institution. The depository institution might provide confirmation after each bill is paid, or send you an itemized record on your monthly statement. There is a charge for each transaction, as much as or less than the charge for using a check.

Direct-deposit accounts Paychecks, Social Security payments, and income from other regularly recurring sources can be deposited directly into your interest-earning transactions account.

Money-market fund accounts Some money-market funds permit checks to be written against your fund account. There is usually a $250 to $500 minimum per check. You earn interest until the check clears.

Asset management accounts Comprehensive financial vehicles built around a money-market fund. They are offered by some large brokerage firms and mutual fund sponsors. Asset management accounts require minimum balances of $5,000 to $20,000, and provide among other services a checking account to which money is transferred from the money-market fund when checks or debit-card transactions are presented for payment.

Debit cards An alternative to check-writing. Debit cards are often described—by those who love them and those who disdain them—as "the advance guard of the 'checkless economy.'" Unlike a credit card, which delays the date on which you pay bills, a debit card authorizes immediate payment from your account to the account of a supermarket or gas station owner or whomever you owe money, in the same or a different depository institution.

Home banking The newest kid on the transactions account block. If you have a personal computer, you may be able to check your account balance, transfer money from one account to another and pay bills without ever leaving home. There is a monthly fee, currently about $8 to $10.

3 Whether a Borrower You Should Be

Do not borrow simply for the sake of establishing a credit record or gaining an interest expense deduction on a tax return. There should be a sound personal motivation for borrowing (buying a house or financing your children's education) or a good economic justification (making an investment that offers the prospect of a good rate of return). It makes sense to borrow only when you feel comfortable undertaking such a commitment, and a loss would not jeopardize your financial security.

Borrowing is included in the financial planning process because the amount you borrow and the terms on which you borrow (interest rate, repayment schedule, maturity of loan) affect the attainment of the long-term goals you set on pages 10-11.

> One of Laura's goals was to return to college. She did not want to wait until she had saved all the money she needed for tuition. She borrowed $1,000 from her savings bank, using her savings account as security for the loan. She thinks this is a good investment in her future.
>
> Peter and Kate have a joint income of $30,000 a year. They want to buy a house, but they cannot get a mortgage. Because they have borrowed so heavily on their bank credit card and are paying off two student loans, the mortgage lender says they do not have adequate income to cover mortgage payments and other housing expenses.

How Much Can You Afford to Borrow?

$$\frac{\$\_\_\_\_\text{(monthly debt repayment)}}{\$\_\_\_\_\text{(one month's pretax income)}} = \_\_\_\_ \%\text{ of monthly income owed to creditors}$$

Is this more, less or about the right amount of debt you can afford to repay now and in the future? If you lost your job or other sources of income, could you raise the cash to pay off your debts? The liquid assets and other marketable assets listed in your Personal Financial Inventory are your sources of such cash.

Where to Borrow

Life insurance policies purchased five years ago or so can be the least expensive source of funds for individual borrowers, with interest rates ranging from 5% to 8%. Some life insurance policies permit their owners to borrow the "cash value," the part of the premium you pay that accumulates somewhat like a savings account. The amount available for borrowing, always less than the amount of insurance that would be paid on the death of the insured person, is found in a table in the policy contract.

There is no requirement to repay the loan, only the interest. However, if the loan remains unpaid and the insured dies, the amount of the loan is deducted from the proceeds the beneficiary receives. You must contact your insurance agent or the insurance company to apply for a policy loan.

Personal loans are offered by banks, S&Ls, credit unions and consumer finance companies for major consumer expenditures like a new car or extensive home improvements. Generally, interest rates on personal loans are lowest at credit unions and highest at finance companies. Personal loans may be *secured* or *unsecured*.

The lender of a secured loan may require the borrower to hand over the title to the property which is being purchased, like a car. Or the *collateral* (the financial asset that secures the loan) may be a savings account, savings certificate, stocks or bonds. If you default on the loan, the lender has the right to use the collateral to pay off the loan. An unsecured loan is made because the lender believes the borrower is both willing and able to repay the loan.

Most personal loans are *installment* loans, which means a part of the loan plus interest is repaid monthly (You may get a lower interest rate if you permit the lender to deduct monthly payments from your checking account). The interest rate on a personal loan may be a *fixed* rate which remains the same throughout the life of the loan, or a *variable* rate which goes up or down as the general level of interest rates goes up or down.

Passbook loans secured by funds in a passbook or statement savings account are offered by savings banks and S&Ls at lower interest rates than rates charged by the same institutions on unsecured personal loans. Borrowers continue to earn interest on their savings, although an amount in the account equal to the amount of the outstanding loan is "frozen" until the loan is repaid. Thus, the real cost of borrowing is the difference between the interest you earn and the interest you pay. (If the loan is secured by a savings certificate, loan rates may be lower *and* the interest earned may be higher.) Most people who borrow rather than use their own savings for a particular expenditure do so because they find it easier to repay a loan than to rebuild their savings nest egg.

Revolving credit is one of the oldest kinds of consumer credit. A customer arranges with a retail store or other vendor to pay off a coat, a refrigerator, or whatever, at a specific rate of interest during a specific period of time. Interest rates on revolving credit purchases are comparable to rates charged on credit card purchases. A maximum allowable interest rate on consumer credit often is set by state law, and varies from state to state.

"Private banking" is a service offered by many large banks to customers whose business is most valued because they are large depositors of the bank and/or have long-term relationships as personal, commercial or trust clients. In addition to receiving prompt attention to their queries and requests, private banking customers often borrow on better terms than other individual borrowers.

Credit-card purchases and cash advances are among the most expensive kinds of consumer credit. A large part of their appeal is that they permit relatively small or odd sums of money to be borrowed at the borrower's discretion. No application or waiting period is required after the account is opened. Credit-card purchases may be paid in full when the monthly bill is presented for payment, or paid off in monthly installments that include an interest charge. The amount of purchases and cash advances permitted is limited to the approved amount on the cardholder's credit line. An annual "membership fee" or monthly service fee may be charged.

Bank credit-card borrowing costs are at the high end of the credit spectrum, to cover the high probability of nonpayment among the least creditworthy cardholders. In addition, some card issuers charge interest not on the previous month's outstanding balance but on the "average daily balance." This calculation includes new purchases you made since the last billing date. Thus, the actual cost of borrowing may be much higher than a stated APR (annual percentage rate).

Unsecured credit lines, like credit-card advances, make a specific amount of credit immediately available at the borrower's discretion. Cash is usually obtained by writing a check on a credit-line checking account. Credit lines offer higher borrowing limits—perhaps $25,000 to $50,000—at lower interest rates than credit-card loans. Part of the outstanding principal balance plus a variable rate of interest is payable monthly. Open credit lines, sometimes labeled "Preferred Credit Lines" or "Executive Credit," are available only to an institution's most credit-worthy customers.

Secured credit lines work on the same principle as unsecured credit lines. However, if the collateral for a secured credit line is a second mortgage on your home, the interest rate might be lower and the payback period longer.

Overdraft privileges share similarities with open credit lines and cash advances. Banks and savings institutions permit customers to "overdraw" their transaction accounts up to an authorized dollar limit. Interest is charged only on borrowed funds, usually at the same rate as credit card advances. The overdraft privilege might be made available only to bank credit-card customers or to all creditworthy transaction-account customers.

Home equity loans permit you to borrow the "equity" in your home; that is, the increase in the value of your ownership in a residence since you bought it. For example, if the current value of your home is $100,000, and you have a $60,000 mortgage, you might be able to borrow as much as 80% of the $40,000 equity, or $32,000, for up to 15 years. Furthermore, money may be taken out by check or credit card when you need it.

Home equity loans are appropriate credit options for such major undertakings as college tuition and large-scale home renovations. Home equity loans should not be used to pay for new stereo systems and Caribbean odysseys. In addition to monthly payments, you may incur closing costs of $200 or more that include a property appraisal, title search, title insurance, lien recording and "points." (Each "point" is equal to one per cent of the amount being borrowed.) Some lenders also charge an annual fee of $25 to $35 to cover administrative costs.

Special-Purpose Borrowing

Student loans to college students and their families are available from the federal government, state government agencies, academic institutions and private lenders. The lowest rates and most liberal repayment terms are on loans made directly to students most in need of financial aid. In 1987, the interest rate on a National Direct Student Loan from the federal government was 5%, with the first payment not due until six months after graduation. The rate on a Guaranteed Student Loan was 8%.

The Parent Loan for Undergraduate Students (PLUS) is a government-guaranteed loan made by private lenders to parents without regard to financial need and at a rate comparable to the prevailing unsecured personal loan rate. The maximum PLUS loan is $4,000, runs ten years and has a 60-day grace period before the first payment is due.

Margin accounts are credit lines at a stock brokerage firm. Customers who buy "on margin" make only partial payment for their purchases of stocks or bonds. They borrow the remainder, typically at a rate 1% to 1.5% above the prime rate (the rate banks charge their most creditworthy customers). The *margin* is the percentage of the purchase the customer must pay. For example, if the margin requirement is 75%, a buyer would put up $3,750 on a $5,000 transaction. The securities purchased are the broker's collateral. If their price rises, the customer benefits from the "leverage" of using borrowed funds. If the value of the securities declines before they are fully paid for or sold by the customer, the broker may call for additional margin.

Credit Life Insurance

Most institutional lenders sell credit life insurance, the proceeds of which are used to pay off a loan if the borrower dies. They are prohibited by the Equal Credit Opportunity Act from making the purchase of credit life insurance a prerequisite for approving your loan.

Before You Apply for a Loan or Credit

• Complete the Personal Income Statement (pages 3-5) and Personal Financial Inventory (pages 6-10). You will be asked for some or all of this information by a lender or credit-card issuer.

WHETHER A BORROWER YOU SHOULD BE

• Keep in mind that if a woman meets credit requirements on her own, lenders and credit-card issuers are not permitted to require husbands or fathers to co-sign for loans.

• Understand that lenders and credit-card issuers must take all sources of income into account—alimony, child support, Social Security, part-time work, investment income, etc.—in evaluating an applicant's creditworthiness.

• Get acquainted with a bank officer where you have your checking or savings account. If someone knows you and is willing to vouch for your good character, it can make the difference between acceptance and rejection when work history and income level are on the borderline for the lender's credit guidelines.

• Comparison shop. Rates and terms vary among lenders.

• Know the real percentage rate at which you borrow. It may be different from the stated rate. For example, your loan may be *discounted*. If you borrow $1,000 at 12% for one year, $120 (12% of $1,000) is deducted immediately. You have the use of only $880 but must repay $1,000. The *effective* or *real rate* is therefore 13.63% ($120 divided by $880 equals $13.63%).

If Your Application is Rejected

Not every application for a loan or credit card is accepted. Prospective borrowers or cardholders must prove they are able and willing to pay their debts. On the other hand, the federal Equal Credit Opportunity Act says that all credit applicants must be judged by the same standards. The Act prohibits discrimination against prospective borrowers because of their age, race or sex.

If you think your application for a loan or credit card was rejected because you are female and that a male counterpart of the same age, income, marital status ane employment record would have received credit:

• Ask why you were rejected. If you are told that the rejection was based on information received from a credit bureau, request a copy of your credit record (see next page).

• Know your rights under the Equal Credit Opportunity Act. Consult a copy of the Act. Every financial institution is required to keep copies for customers' use.

• Ask the loan officer or credit-card company employee to reconsider the decision. Say you are familiar with the Act, and that you believe you were rejected without cause.

• If you receive no satisfaction, write a letter, or ask your attorney to write a letter, to the president of the organization that rejected your application. Send a copy of the letter to your state or local department of consumer affairs. Make certain that the head of the lending institution knows you are sending this copy.

• If you still receive no satisfaction, ask the state or local department of consumer affairs for help.

• As a last resort, ask for the name of the state or federal regulatory agency with regulatory responsibility for the organization that rejected your application. File a complaint with that agency.

How to Check Your Credit Record

If you have credit cards or outstanding loans, your credit history is probably on file at a local credit bureau. The information in your file is supplied by the organizations that have extended credit to you, such as banks and retail stores. If you are curious about the information the bureau is disclosing about you, you may request a copy of your file.

Ask your bank for the name of the local credit bureau it uses. Call the credit bureau and request a file disclosure form. There is no fee for the form if you have been denied credit within the past thirty days; otherwise, a small fee is charged. Fill out and return the file disclosure form.

You will receive a credit report with the following information (usually in barely decipherable computerese):

A list of past and current debts.

How quickly you pay your bills.

Whether and why you have been refused credit.

Whether you have declared bankruptcy.
Whether you are delinquent or have defaulted on a student loan.
Any experiences with creditors' attorneys or collection agencies.
Other information filed by and of interest to creditors.

Inform the credit bureau in writing if inaccurate information appears on your credit report. The bureau is supposed to confirm your contention and make the necessary changes on your record.

Apply for another credit report to make certain it's been done.

Why a Married Woman Should Have A Credit Record in Her Own Name

No one should borrow or get a credit card simply for the sake of establishing a credit record. But if a married woman has legitimate need for a loan or a credit card, there are several reasons why she, even with no income of her own, should establish an independent financial identity.

The grim statistics There were 26.6 million widows and divorcees in the U.S. in 1985. Only 40% of women widowed in their thirties, 19% of women widowed in their forties, 9% of women widowed in their fifties, and 5% of widows sixty years old or older remarry. Of all married women, 85% will be widowed or divorced.

If you are widowed or divorced and have had financial accounts in your own name, you are spared the burden of closing old accounts and opening new ones under emotionally trying circumstances. If you have no previous credit record or if your income as a single woman is lower than it was as a married woman, your credit application for a new account might be rejected.

The best way to learn is by doing If it's *your* bank account or credit card, it's *your* responsibility. You are more likely to monitor and actively manage financial matters than to "let George do it."

Control over your financial well-being Nobody, not even a kind and generous husband, looks out for your money as well as you do yourself. In fact, many men have neither the time nor the interest in active money management and keeping up with new financial services. Women who are experienced family budgeters quickly learn to deal with financial institutions the same way they deal with vendors of other goods and services: searching out and getting the best possible service at the best possible price.

To Establish Your Credit Rating

• Open your own checking and savings account or an interest-paying transaction account. Make a passbook loan from your savings account. Have credit cards imprinted with your own name.

• Request that credit records for joint accounts be kept for you separately from your husband's. As an individual account-holder, even a woman who has no income of her own may establish a track record as a reliable and responsible borrower. The *willingness* to repay closely follows the *ability* to repay as a requirement for good credit risks.

• Apply for an open credit line or overdraft privilege on your checking account. This is the easiest credit to get if you have no previous credit record but are known by someone at the branch at which you bank.

• Use the credit line for a substantial expenditure, such as a college tuition payment or new living-room furniture. The money to pay the college or the furniture store might come from your husband, but *you* get the Brownie points for repaying the loan.

• If income-producing assets, such as stocks, bonds, or savings accounts, can be transferred from your husband or a joint account to your name alone, you might have adequate income to qualify for your own bank credit card, retail-store account, or gasoline credit card.

4 Nobody Knows What's Coming Tomorrow: Life, Disability and Health Insurance*

Why buy life insurance? The more dependent others are on you and the less other assets you have, the more life insurance you need. The less dependent others are on you and the more other assets you have, the less life insurance you need.

Whether you buy life insurance, and the amount you buy, depends on how you would want the proceeds of the policy to be used.

> Judith is divorced and the mother of 12-year-old twins. While her ex-husband contributes to the children's support, she is not certain he would be willing to pay their college tuitions if she were not around to pay a share. Judith uses insurance to assure her children of the education she wants them to have.
>
> Harriet is single and has no dependents, but in the future she might have to supplement her widowed mother's income from a small pension and Social Security. An insurance policy on Harriet's life will provide that additional income if her mother outlives Harriet.
>
> Tom and Elaine are able to purchase a condominium only because they have two incomes to pay off the mortgage. If one of them dies, the other will be forced to sell the apartment. They have insurance for the specific purpose of keeping a roof over the head of a surviving spouse.

---

*Property and liability insurance are not discussed in this workbook. However, if you own property which is insurable against loss, theft or damage, such as a car or house, or if you could be held responsible (i.e., liable) for other persons being injured or their property damaged, then you should investigate and buy the appropriate insurance coverage.

CALCULATE YOUR LIFE-INSURANCE NEEDS

Life insurance is needed for two kinds of financial obligations: (1) one-time lump-sum expenditures and (2) on-going income. Estimate what your lump sum and income needs might be according to your current situation.

ONE-TIME LUMP-SUM EXPENDITURES

Final expenses [1]
    (funeral, non-covered
    medical, legal and taxes) $_____
Household bills and loans   _____
Optional Mortgage Cancellation Fund [2]   _____
Four years' college tuition [3] for

_____   _____
_____   _____
_____   _____
_____   _____

Other

_____   _____
_____   _____
_____   _____
_____   _____

TOTAL LUMP SUM NEEDS $_____

TOTAL FUNDS AVAILABLE TO COVER
LUMP-SUM NEEDS
Life insurance currently owned   _____
Financial assets [4]   _____

TOTAL SOURCES OF FUNDS $_____

EXCESS FUNDS AVAILABLE FOR INVESTMENT [5] $_____
    or
ADDITIONAL INSURANCE NEEDED
TO COVER LUMP-SUM NEEDS $_____

LIFE, DISABILITY AND HEALTH INSURANCE

SURVIVORS' ANNUAL INCOME NEEDS (6) $_____
    less
SOURCES OF ANNUAL INCOME
Salary $_____
Social Security   _____
Annuities   _____
Income* from investments (7)   _____
Pension (8)   _____

TOTAL ESTIMATED INCOME $_____
    equals
ADDITIONAL INCOME TO BE GENERATED (9) $_____

INSURANCE NEEDED
TO GENERATED ADDITIONAL INCOME (10) $_____

TOTAL INSURANCE THAT MIGHT BE NEEDED
TO COVER LUMP-SUM NEEDS AND
GENERATE ADDITIONAL INCOME (11) $_____

*Assume 8% could be earned on currently owned investments and investible insurance proceeds.

Guide to Calculating Your Life-Insurance Needs

(1) "Final expenses" is obviously an estimated figure. For smaller estates—less than $100,000—legal expenses and taxes are minimal, so $5,000 should cover funeral and non-reimbursable medical costs. Final expenses for large estates—over $500,000—are at least $10,000. Expenses for medium-sized estates fall somewhere in between.

(2) An "optional mortgage cancellation fund" gives a surviving spouse or other family members flexibility regarding on-going mortgage payments. Enter the outstanding balance on your current mortgage.

(3) For "college tuition" use current costs for both current and future students. You don't need to have in hand now four years worth of tuition that isn't due to begin until five or ten years from now, but the total figure gives you an approximation of your future obligations.

(4) "Financial assets," for the purpose of this calculation, are your total assets less residences, personal property and a surviving spouse's retirement benefits.

(5) Your one-time lump sum needs might be greater than funds currently available to cover them. If so, then "excess funds available for investment" becomes "additional insurance needed to cover lump sum needs."

(6) "Survivors' annual income needs" is some percentage of your family's annual personal and household expenditures with one less family member to account for. For example, if a family of four has been living comfortably on $40,000, its expenses might fall to $30,000 after the loss of a member.

(7) "Income from investments" is derived from currently owned financial assets, including life insurance but excluding a surviving spouse's retirement benefits. An 8% return is suggested for calculating potential investment income because it is a rate that has been atttainable on relatively low-risk, high-quality investments in recent years.

(8) "Pension" can be either a surviving spouse's own pension or retirement benefits provided by the deceased spouse's employer.

(9) "Additional income to be generated" is the difference between the annual income you think will be needed after the death of a family breadwinner and the income that will be available from salaries, investments, Social Security and retirement benefits.

(10) Divide "additional income to be generated" by 8% and multiply by 1,000. For example, if your family needs $15,000 additional income, the amount of life insurance that would generate $15,000, invested to earn 8%, is $187,500.

(11) Add your estimate of additional insurance needed to cover lump-sum needs and insurance needed to generate additional income. This is the amount of insurance you might need to fullfill your current responsibilities. *As your financial assets increase in value and your responsibilities to others diminish, you will need less life insurance.*

What Kind of Life Insurance Should You Buy?

Usually, you should buy the most insurance coverage for the least amount of money over the time period you think you will need insurance. You want to deal only with reputable, well-capitalized companies willing and able to pay up if the need arises. The most financially stable carriers are rated A+ or A in the directory of insurers published by A. M. Best & Company. This book may be found in the reference section of most public libraries.

Life-insurance proceeds are paid to beneficiaries when an insured person dies. Some policies combine savings with death benefits; that is, if the insured person lives to a certain age, he or she receives a lump sum or periodic payments.

Do not purchase life insurance as an investment. In the long run, if you follow a regular program and invest sensibly, you probably will earn a better rate of return than using the same money to pay premiums on life insurance which includes a savings component.

Do purchase life insurance as protection for the people dependent on you for financial support. The advantage of life insurance over other investments is that the proceeds will be paid to your beneficiaries if you die before you have had the time to accumulate the funds you want for specific goals.

Some life-insurance policy owners, if informed that equal or better coverage is available at a lower price, will claim "I can't turn in my policy. I've had it too long." Unless a policy holder has become uninsurable or is in a high-risk category (i.e., diabetics, cigarette smokers), there usually is nothing to be gained by holding onto a costly policy bought ten or fifteen years ago when the life-insurance business was considerably less competitive. The bottom line on life insurance is: shop around.

The two main kinds of life insurance are term *and* whole life. *Several variations of whole life, such as* universal life *and* variable life, *have been introduced in recent years.*

Term insurance As the name implies, term insurance provides insurance coverage for a specific period of time—one year, five years, ten years. Annual payments for term insurance are less expensive than whole life in our younger years and more expensive in our older years. However, during the years most people have the greatest need for insurance, the total cost of term premiums tends to be lower than the total cost of whole life premiums.*

Term policies are not automatically renewed each time a coverage period ends. Therefore, there is the risk that an insured person who has become "uninsurable" since the policy went into effect will not qualify for continued coverage. To protect yourself against this possibility, pay a small additional charge for a *guaranteed renewable and convertible policy.* The renewability clause eliminates the need to prove insurability again. The convertibility clause allows someone who has become uninsurable the option of converting a term policy to permanent long-term coverage.

Group insurance policies provided as employee benefits are term policies. Coverage usually ends when an employee leaves the company. Ex-employees often are given the option by their firm's insurer to purchase a whole life policy for the same amount of coverage without a medical examination. However, conversion rates are often more expensive than similar coverage that can be purchased elsewhere. If you are healthy, it may be cheaper to buy a new policy than to convert.

Decreasing term insurance A variety of term insurance often purchased as mortgage insurance on a home or as tuition insurance for a child's education is called decreasing term insurance. The amount that would be paid to beneficiaries of a decreasing term policy declines as the outstanding value of the mortgage or tuition obligation decreases. If the insured dies before the mortgage is repaid or the child's education completed, the policy proceeds are used to pay off the mortgage or remaining tuition.

A decreasing term policy intended as mortgage insurance should be written as a general policy so that a surviving spouse or other beneficiaries have the option to pay off the mortgage. If current interest rates are higher than the mortgage rate, the beneficiaries might want to invest the insurance proceeds and continue to make mortgage payments.

Whole life insurance When you buy a whole life insurance policy—also known as "permanent life," "straight life" or "ordinary life"—you are insured from the day the policy begins to the day you die. Premiums may be paid throughout your lifetime or for a limited time period, such as ten or twenty years.

*The "premium" is not something that comes in a crackerjack box. It is your payment to the insurance company for the insurance coverage it provides. Premiums may be paid monthly, quarterly, semiannually or once a year.

LIFE, DISABILITY AND HEALTH INSURANCE

A small percentage of the premiums you pay for whole life coverage accumulates somewhat like a savings account. This is called the *cash value*. A whole life policy owner gets the cash value only if he or she terminates the policy or makes a loan. If the insured dies, beneficiaries get only the amount of insurance purchased but no cash value unless special provision has been made to "insure" the cash value. There is never a cash value build-up with a term policy.

You may borrow the cash value in your whole life policy at any time, often at lower interest rates than are available from other credit sources (see page 20). However, if the loan remains unpaid and the insured dies, the benefits of the policy decrease by the amount borrowed.

Cash and loan values for each year you own a policy are printed in the "Table of Cash, Loan and Other Values" in all whole life contracts.

Individuals who no longer need their current amount of whole life coverage have three options if they wish to lower or stop paying premiums:

• Terminating the policy by withdrawing the cash value and investing the proceeds at higher rates of interest than the insurance company pays.

• Limiting the time period the policy remains in effect, the "term" depending on the cash value available to cover future premiums.

• Converting to paid-up whole life. The policy continues, but at a lower face value (lower benefits to beneficiaries). No further premium payments are due.

When is a Dividend Not a Dividend?

The customary definition of a "dividend" is "the distribution of profits to shareholders of a corporation." However, insurance companies also pay "dividends," which are partial refunds on premiums paid on insurance policies called "participating" policies.

The companies justify the return of overpayments by claiming that their costs were lower than anticipated during the preceding premium payment period. In the interim, they have had the use of millions of dollars of interest-free loans.

Naming the Players:
Owners and Beneficiaries

The *owner* of a life insurance policy is the person who has the *rights of ownership:* to assign (transfer ownership of) the policy to another person; to name or change beneficiaries; to terminate the policy; to withdraw the cash value; to borrow the cash value; and to change the premium payment period (whether premiums should be paid monthly, quarterly or yearly).

The owner of an insurance policy might be, but does not have to be, the person whose life is insured by the policy (the insured).

Also, the owner of the policy might be the same or different from the policy's *beneficiary,* the person who receives the proceeds of the policy upon the death of the insured. *Named beneficiaries are not required to pay income tax on life-insurance proceeds.*

Before 1982, husbands and wives often were advised to transfer ownership of their insurance policies to their spouses so that the proceeds would not be subject to federal death taxes. As a result of a 1981 change in the tax law, spouses now are able to bequeath an unlimited amount of assets to their husbands and wives free of federal estate tax. Under these circumstances, a married woman taking out insurance for the first time might want to retain ownership of her policy during her lifetime and bequeath it to her husband in her will.

Divorced women are advised to protect their alimony payments by receiving as part of their divorce settlements ownership of an insurance policy on their husband's lives. The face value of the policy should be an amount that could generate the income the ex-spouse will provide during his lifetime. For example, if alimony is $20,000 a year, insurance should be at least $250,000, assuming that 8% could be earned on investments. The funds to pay the premium on the policy should be provided in addition to, not as part of, alimony.

Payment of Life-
Insurance Proceeds

Either the owner or the beneficiary of an insurance policy decides how the proceeds of a policy will be paid to the beneficiary. The two choices—called *settlement options*—are either to receive a lump-sum distribution or periodic payments.

The advantage of a lump-sum distribution is that the beneficiary has immediate control and use of the funds. Money may be used for pressing personal needs, invested, or used to pay estate settlement expenses, such as taxes or lawyers' fees.

If periodic payments are elected, the insurance company pays interest on the undistributed portion of the proceeds, but often at a lower rate than the beneficiary could earn on her own by investing in savings instruments (Chapter 2) or bonds (Chapter 5). Also, if a periodic payment option is chosen, and the beneficiary dies before the final distribution is made, some companies reduce the rate of interest paid to the beneficiary's beneficiaries.

If You Are Married and the Beneficiary of Your Husband's Insurance Policy, Remember

• Many widows who receive insurance payments are bombarded by fast-talking sales people offering "golden investment opportunities" that must be taken advantage of immediately. Stockbrokers and well-meaning friends also will call with advice about "what you should do with your money."

• Do nothing which you might later regret. No important financial decisions should be made under such difficult emotional circumstances as the recent death of a husband. The best thing a widow can do with an insurance payment is put it in a safe, liquid savings instrument until she feels ready to think clearly and rationally about her long-term needs.

How To Apply for Payment of a Life-Insurance Policy

• If you have the responsibility of collecting life-insurance proceeds, contact the insurance agent who sold the policy. He or she should be able to guide you through the collection process.

• If you do not know the agent, write directly to the insurance company. The name and address is printed on the policy. Request an insurance claim application, providing the decedent's name, a copy of the death certificate, the policy number, and your name and address.

• You will receive a form which must be signed by the policy's beneficiary. If the owner has provided the option, the form will ask the beneficiary to choose between a lump-sum or periodic-payment distribution.

• Keep copies of all correspondence with the insurance company.

• A check for the lump-sum payment or the first installment payment should arrive three to five weeks after the claim is filed.

• If you have any problems or feel that the company is not handling your claim properly, contact the regulatory agency for insurance in your state.

Do Not Buy

• Life insurance at airports. The possibility of dying in an airplane accident does not determine your insurance needs; family and financial position does.

• Life insurance on children. The primary purpose of insurance is to replace income lost by the death of a breadwinner. Few children are the source of their family's financial sustenance.

Disability Insurance

The chances of being incapacitated and unable to work are higher than the probability of death at every age level for pre-retirement-age workers.*

When Patsy the Plumber or Nancy the Nurse has an accident or long-term illness, her income goes *down* and her expenses go *up*. The purpose of disability insurance is to replace income you no longer are able to earn on your own.

* A woman must be employed outside the home to be covered by disability insurance. If you're a homemaker with two small children and break your leg, no matter how expensive it will be to replace your services, you will not qualify. The best you can do is make certain your husband is insured, and watch where you walk.

How is Disability Defined?

Different insurance companies define "disability" differently and make disability payments under different circumstances.

Definition 1 Unable to work at *any* occupation. Translation: If an injured ballet dancer can sell pencils from a chair on a streetcorner, she is not disabled.

Definition 2 Unable to perform the duties of any *gainful* occupation for which you are reasonably qualified. Translation: If the injured ballerina can teach in a dancing school, she is not disabled.

Definition 3 Unable to perform the "substantial and material duties" of your regular occupation. Translation: If the injured ballerina cannot dance in performances with her company, she *is* disabled.

The best disability coverage is number three.

When Should Disability Payments Begin and How Long Should They Last?

The sooner payments begin after a disabling event, the more expensive the policy. The longer the period of coverage, the more expensive the policy.

Recommended: Disability payments that begin three months after a worker is incapacitated and continue for life or to age sixty-five. One of the best reasons to have a savings nest egg (page 12) is to be able to "self-insure" until disability payments begin.

How Much Disability Income Do You Need?

No insurer will commit itself to replacing 100% of your earned income; the possibility of taking "early retirement" on disability income is considered too great an incentive not to work. *Sixty percent of your current after-tax income* is a realistic minimum to receive, considering the high cost of disability coverage and the fact that disability income is not taxable if you pay the premiums. (If your employer pays the premiums, payments are considered taxable income to the recipient.)

What Kind of Health Insurance Do You Need?

Basic coverage should pay for all or a large part of inpatient and outpatient surgical procedures, diagnostic services, laboratory tests, room, meals, nurses, medication, etc., during a hospital stay. The amount of the bill that you pay is called the "deductible." The higher the deductible, the lower the premium.

Major medical is a supplement to basic coverage for costly long-term illnesses. It pays all medical costs but the "deductible" up to a high lifetime maximum. Because of the enormous expense of such procedures as open-heart surgery, a major medical lifetime maximum of $200,000 to $500,000 is suggested.

Medicare Part A is a basic hospital insurance plan offered at no charge to Social Security recipients sixty-five years old and older and the long-term disabled of any age. Medicare pays all hospital costs, less a specified deductible, for the first sixty days of hospitalization and all costs less a "co-pay" (what you pay) for the next thirty days. There is a lifetime sixty-day reserve with a "co-pay" twice the amount of the previous time period. Medicare A covers skilled nursing care for a limited period in a nursing home or at home after a hospital stay, physical, occupational and speech therapy, and hospice care.

Medicare Part B is available for a monthly premium ($17.90 in 1987) and pays, after a $75 deductible, 80% of physicians' services considered "reasonable" by the government. Among other costs, Medicare Part B pays for X-rays, home dialysis supplies and equipment, the rental or purchase of wheelchairs, and up to $250 of psychiatric care.

Medigap refers to health insurance policies issued by private companies that pay all or part of many expenses not covered by Medicare, such as deductibles and co-payments, hospital costs beyond the 91st day of hospitalization, private duty nursing care, nursing home care from the 21st day of occupancy to the 365th, and prescription drugs. Medigap is a supplement to, not a replacement for, Medicare.

Long-term custodial care is not covered by Medicare, Medigap or most traditional health insurance policies. Policies for the specific purpose of defraying all or part of the cost of residential care or a long-term stay in a nursing home have been introduced by some major insurers, such as Aetna, Metropolitan Life, Prudential and United Equitable. Although the policies have stringent criteria before a stream of payments begins, they offer some relief to the middle-class elderly whose lifetime savings can be quickly dissipated by a year or two in a nursing home.

What Kind of Health Insurance Do You Have?

Individual health insurance is insurance you purchase on your own. You may have more flexibility in tailoring coverage to your particular needs and pocketbook when you, rather than an employer, are paying premiums. On the other hand, insurance purchased by one person is almost always more expensive than the same coverage purchased by a large organization for many participants. One exception is the non-group plan offered at reduced rates by some private health insurers to lower- and lower-middle-income earners.

The premiums you pay for health-care insurance could be a tax deductible expense (See Chapter 15).

Group health insurance is provided through places of employment, unions, professional groups and trade associations. One advantage of group insurance is the "quantity discount" given by the insurer to a large entity. Another, if you are an employee, is having your employer pay the premium without its cost being considered taxable income to you.

Legislation recently passed by Congress requires all employers with twenty or more employees who maintain health-insurance plans to permit certain individuals who had been covered by the plan but no longer have an affiliation with the sponsoring organization to remain on the health plan for three years after departure. Ex-spouses, surviving spouses of deceased employees, employees who have been fired for reasons other than gross misconduct and children who no longer qualify as dependents may take advantage of this option. The law permits an employer to pass on the cost of continued coverage to any individual electing such coverage.

Pre-existing condition clauses are included in most private health-insurance policies. They exempt an insurance company from covering a new subscriber—individual or group-plan participant—for an illness, an injury or a condition such as pregnancy that existed before the individual joined the plan. If you transfer coverage from an employer's plan to *your own plan or another employer's plan with the same insurance company* you may be exempt from the pre-existing condition restriction.

Health Maintenance Organizations (HMOs) are a medical-care option through which individuals and employers pay a flat annual fee for the services listed above as basic coverage and major medical. Most HMOs require members to use only hospitals and doctors affiliated with the HMO.

Do Not Buy

'Dread' disease insurance. If you and your family need health insurance, you need it to defray expenses incurred from *all* kinds of catastrophic illnesses, not just specific ones such as cancer or heart disease.

5 Taking Stock of Stocks and Bonds

In Chapter 1, you set down your financial goals (retirement income, cutting your tax bill, children's education fund, etc.). The next seven chapters introduce you to the investments that will help you reach those goals.

Stocks and bonds are the traditional investments most people use to provide income and make their money grow over long periods of time.

If you buy **stock**, you are an *owner* and have an *equity* interest in a company. Investors in a company's *common* stock expect to share in its financial success through quarterly *dividends* and an increase in the price of their stock. Investors in a company's *preferred* stock resemble *creditors* more than equity owners; they receive a specific dividend, stated as a percentage of the issue price or number of dollars, such as 9% or $4.00. Dividends are paid on preferred stock before any dividends are paid on common stock. The kind of stock referred to when you hear that "XYZ Corporation's stock" or "the stock market" went up or down is *common* stock.

Bonds are IOUs issued by large corporations, cities, states and the U.S. government. If you buy a bond, you are a *creditor* of the corporate or government issuer. Bonds pay *interest*—usually twice a year—to the bondholders.

Why Buy Stocks and Bonds?

Ten years ago, JoAnn and Charles started an investment program for their daughter's education with $2,000. They bought common stock with the expectation that the stock would increase in value as the issuing companies prospered. Through judicious buying and selling and reinvesting dividends in additional shares, JoAnn and Charles accumulated a fund large enough to cover the tuition bills that now arrive regularly twice a year.

Marcia, on the other hand, wants additional income to supplement her schoolteacher's salary. With $5,000 to invest, she bought government bonds. They are safe and can be counted on to pay 9% interest, or $450, each year. Marcia knows she might earn a higher rate of interest on a corporate bond, or perhaps double her money on a "hot tip" in the stock market, but she feels she cannot afford to risk losing any of the money she has taken so long to accumulate.

The Risk-Return Trade-Off

Because stock and bond prices go up and down, there is more *risk* that you might lose your money than if you bought a savings certificate or money market fund. However, there also is the prospect of a higher *return*.

In general, the higher the *expected return* on an investment, the greater the *possibility of loss* on that investment.

Everyone has her own level of tolerance for risk. Ask yourself:
- If I make this investment, will I be able to sleep at night?
- If I lose money on this investment, will it *significantly* affect my current spending and plans for the future?

Only you can answer these questions. Only *you* know what's right for *you*, and what's right for you is different from what's right for your sister-in-law, your best friend, your hairdresser or your stockbroker.

Ask yourself these questions before every investment decision you make. If you answer "yes" to the first question and "no" to the second, you will have the opportunity for greater gain than if you make only relatively low-risk investments.

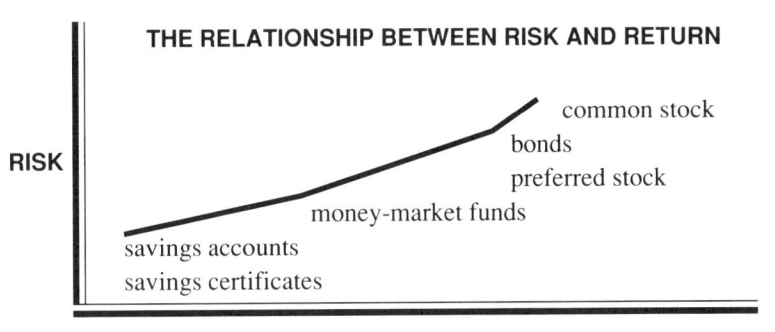

THE RELATIONSHIP BETWEEN RISK AND RETURN

RISK

common stock
bonds
preferred stock
money-market funds
savings accounts
savings certificates

EXPECTED RETURN

TAKING STOCK OF STOCKS AND BONDS

Choosing Stocks for Different Financial Goals

Income stocks are issued by companies such as public utilities which have a history of paying high dividends to their shareholders. Should be bought by investors who want to earn current income and who have a low tolerance for risk.

Blue-chip stocks are issued by long-established and well-known companies about which information is easily obtained; their familiarity as "household names" make investors feel safe buying their stock. Should be bought by investors who want a combination of income and growth and who have a low to medium tolerance for risk.

Growth stocks are issued by rapidly growing companies that reinvest all or almost all their earnings in the company and pay low or no dividends. A shareholder's return comes from the expectation that the stock's price will rise as the company prospers. Should be bought by investors who do not need current income and have a medium to high tolerance for risk.

Speculative stocks are the opposite of "blue chip"; they are issued by a young, untested company in a high-growth industry with a unique product, or an older company recovering from a period of severe financial reversals. Should be bought by investors who do not need current income and have a high tolerance for risk.

How To Pick A Stock

First ask, "what is my objective?" Is it "growth," like JoAnn and Charles? Or "income," like Marcia?

If it's growth, choose an *industry* with *high growth potential*. This means identifying companies whose products and service people are buying and using in large amounts *and* whose sales are likely to continue to grow.

Choose a *leading company* in that industry. Look for the firm that's introducing successful new products, the company with a reputation for being aggressive and innovative.

Whether it's growth or income, look for *good management*. Firms that are well managed usually are firms that make money for their shareholders.

Whether it's growth or income, investigate the company's *financial status*. Make certain that current earnings are adequate to cover dividend payments and interest due on company borrowings (bank loan and bonds). Ask your stockbroker or go to the library for a recent financial report in a publication such as the Value Line Investment Survey or Standard and Poor's Investment Outlook.

Pay attention to your stock! Common stock is not like a savings certificate, something to put in a drawer and make a note on the calendar to renew in six months. Follow your stock in the newspaper, read all reports sent by the company, check it out periodically in an investment service subscribed to by your local library, such as the *Value Line Investment Survey*. Paying attention is the most essential ingredient in any effective money making formula.

The Effect of Inflationary Expectations on the Purchase of Growth and Income Stocks

Inflation describes a time period—usually several years—during which prices of consumer goods, personal services and business services rise steeply and continuously.

When inflation is expected to persist, one way investors try to protect the purchasing power of their dollars is by buying assets that have the potential to increase in value, such as "growth" stocks and real estate. Another is to invest in "income stocks" of companies with earnings more than adequate to raise dividend rates to keep up with the rate of inflation.

Five Ways to Become A Stockholder

• Be an individual investor (see above).
• Buy shares in a mutual fund (see Chapter 6).
• Start an investment club with a group of friends. Each member makes a monthly contribution to an investment "kitty." Members take turns doing

research and recommending stocks for the club to buy. Some clubs have a stockbroker act as an adviser and assist members with their stock selections.

For more information about investment clubs, write to:
National Association of Investment Clubs
1515 East Eleven Mile Road
Royal Oak, Michigan 48067

• Participate in your employer's stock-purchase plan. This can be done by buying a few shares at a time, through periodic payroll deductions, or electing to have some of your retirement-plan distributions invested in company stock.

• Some corporations provide stock options to their employees which permit purchases at less than the market price of the company stock. If you are able to purchase stock for $30 a share that is worth $50 a share, you will have a profit of $20 a share if you sell it.

How to Read
The Stock-Market Page

- Know whether the stock you are interested in is listed on the New York Stock Exchange, the American Stock Exchange or the Over-the-Counter Market (OTC).
- The stock will be listed in alphabetical order but abbreviated in tiny letters. **Disney** is Walt Disney Productions. **DowCh** is Dow Chemical.
- If a company's name is listed with no letters following, it is the company's *common stock*.
- If a company's name is listed with **pf** following, it is the company's *preferred stock*.
- If you want to know the most recent price per share of a stock, look at the figure in the **Close** column. **DukeP** (Duke Power, a public utility company), closed at **44 1/2**, or $44.50 per share, the last price paid for a share the preceding day. The **High** and **Low** are the price range of shares purchased that day.
- You might want to compare a stock's current price with its high and low during the past year (**52 Weeks**). Changes in a stock's price may reflect not only how investors value this stock relative to all other stocks, but also a rising or falling trend of prices in the stock market.
- Does the company pay a *dividend*? Dividends usually are paid quarterly to the shareholders. **DaytHd** (Dayton Hudson, a department store chain) is currently paying an annual dividend of 92 cents per share, or 23 cents per share every three months.
- The *current yield* of a stock is the annual dividend represented as a *percentage* of the previous day's closing price. Dayton Hudson's current yield is 1.6% and **DetEd** (Detroit Edison, another public utility) is 11.5%. The first is a *growth* stock, purchased by investors who do not want current income but expect to profit from a rise in the company's stock. The latter is an *income* stock, purchased by investors who are less interested in the prospect of capital appreciation in the future than income they can depend on and spend now.
- A company's **PE** (price-earnings) **Ratio** indicates investor expectations of its future profitability compared with other companies. A stock's previous day's closing price is divided by the company's after-tax profits per share to attain its PE.
- **Sales 100s** is an abbreviated report of the number of shares of a stock "traded" (bought and sold) the previous day. Dayton Hudson's 21038 indicates sales of 21,038,000 shares. When a **z** precedes the sales figure it is an actual number; i.e., only 100 shares of **DetEd pf 9.32** were sold.

TAKING STOCK OF STOCKS AND BONDS

NEW YORK STOCK EXCHANGE COMPOSITE TRANSACTIONS

52 Weeks High	Low	Stock	Div.	Yld %	P-E Ratio	Sales 100s	High	Low	Close	Net Chg.
— D — D — D —
29⅞	17⅜	DCNY s	.10i	.6	13	128	17⅝d	17¼	17¼	— ½
29¼	22¾	DPL	2.08	8.4	8	193	25	24⅝	24⅝	— ⅛
15⅝	12½	Dallas	.66	4.8	275	3	13¾	13¾	13¾	— ¼
18	7¾	DamnC s	...	...		129	16⅞	16⅛	16⅛	— ⅛
54¼	27⅜	DanaCp	1.44	2.8	27	2263	52⅛	51⅝	51⅝	...
15⅝	5⅛	Danhr s	...	...	26	358	14½	14¼	14¼	...
13⅞	6⅜	Daniel	.18	1.7	...	92	10½	10½	10½	...
38¾	25	DataGn	...	...		764	31⅛	30½	30⅞	+ ⅜
8⅞	4⅝	Datapt	...	...		658	8⅛	8	8	...
33	21½	Datpt pf	4.94	16.4	...	6	30⅛	30	30⅛	— ⅛
8⅞	5¼	DtaDsg	.24	2.9	8	51	8⅝	8⅜	8⅜	...
25½	9⅛	DavWtr	.16	1.1	16	53	15¼	15	15⅛	+ ⅛
63	38¾	DaytHd	.92	1.6	17	21038	59⅛	57⅛	57¼	— ¾
93⅜	76¼	DPL pf	7.70	10.0	...	z20	77½	77	77	— ½
38½	25¾	DeanFd	.54	1.7	21	245	33¾	32	32	— ¾
12⅝	7	DIC	...	...	29	344	11½	11¼	11⅜	...
37⅝	22¼	Deere	.25	.7	...	4642	37⅛	36⅝	36⅝	...
22	18¾	DelVal	1.80	8.8	11	11	20⅝	20⅜	20⅜	...
23⅜	18¼	DelmP s	1.41	7.5	10	664	19	18¾	18¾	— ⅛
67⅛	42⅞	DeltaAr	1.20	2.4	9	2432	51⅛	50½	50½	...
6⅞	4⅞	Deltona	...	...	46	30	5½	5¼	5½	...
42¼	27⅞	DlxChk	.80	2.3	23	1074	35⅝	34⅜	34⅜	— 1
35½	26½	DensMf	1.24	3.8	14	125	33	32½	32½	— ⅝
43¾	36⅞	DeSoto	1.40	3.6	18	86	39⅜	38⅝	38⅝	— ½
19	14⅝	DetEd	1.68	11.5	5	4155	14⅞	14⅝	14⅝	— ⅛
99	88	DetE pf	9.32	10.6	...	z100	88	88	88	...
27⅜	25⅜	DE pfF	2.75	10.8	...	7	25½d	25¼	25½	— ½
30¼	27	DE prR	3.24	11.8	...	24	27⅝	27½	27½	— ¼
29⅜	26⅛	DE pfQ	3.13	11.5	...	39	27⅛	27	27⅛	...
29⅜	26¼	DE pfP	3.12	11.8	...	5	26½	26¼	26½	— ¼
29	24⅞	DE pfB	2.75	10.9	...	5	25¼	24⅞	25⅛	...
31¼	27¼	DE prO	3.40	12.3	...	8	27¾	27½	27¾	+ ¼
30¾	27⅜	DE pfM	3.42	12.6	...	53	27¾d	27¼	27¼	— ⅜
25⅞	22¼	DetE pr	2.28	9.7	...	2	23¾	23½	23½	— ½
30¼	18⅜	Dexter s	.60	2.1	18	201	28⅞	28⅜	28⅜	— ⅜
32¼	20⅞	DiGior	.64	2.6	...	989	25½	24½	25	+ ¼
20½	14⅞	DiaSO	2.80	15.1	...	195	19	18⅛	18½	— ¼
18¼	14⅝	DShRM n	.40	2.7	...	565	14⅞	14⅝	14⅝	— ¼
13¾	10	DianaCp	.30	2.5	14	11	12⅛	12	12	+ ⅛
60¾	37½	Diebold	1.20	2.4	20	753	50¼	49⅛	49⅛	— ½
198½	88⅛	Digital	...	...	21	7968	188⅞	182¼	182½	— 5
82½	36	Disney	.32	.4	26	3616	74⅝	72⅝	72¾	— 1⅛
29⅞	21	DEI	1.48	5.2	23	337	29¾	28½	28½	— 1⅛
7⅜	4¾	DivrsIn	...	...		117	5⅞	5¾	5¾	— ¼
49⅞	39½	DomRs	2.96	7.2	9	1781	42⅛	41	41¼	— ¼
45	32½	Donald	.66	1.6	17	6	40¾	40¾	40¾	— ¼
45⅜	29½	Donley s	.70	1.8	19	696	40	39½	39⅝	+ ⅛
76½	39⅞	Dover	1.12	1.6	28	302	74	72	72	— ⅞
104⅜	51⅛	DowCh	2.20	2.3	21	6982	100¼	97½	97¾	— ¼
56¼	31⅞	DowJns	.64	1.4	23	1091	48¼	45⅜	45¾	— 2
22⅞	17	Downey	.36	1.9	5	9	18⅝	18⅝	18⅝	+ ¼
21⅞	15½	Dravo	.25j	...	37	110	19⅜	19	19	— ¼
35⅝	17⅝	Dresr	.40	1.2	...	945	32⅝	32⅜	32⅝	...
25½	18⅝	DrexB	1.86	9.2	...	16	20½	20¼	20¼	— ⅛
45½	23⅞	Dreyfus	.48	1.5	15	518	31¾	31¼	31¼	— ⅛
131	77¾	duPont	3.40	3.1	17	7052	113⅜	110½	110¾	— ½
53½	43½	duPnt pf	3.50	7.9	...	22	44¼	44¼	44¼	...
66	56	duPnt pf	4.50	7.7	...	51	58⅞	58¼	58¼	— ½
10⅞	8¼	DufPh n	.55e	6.7	...	2078	8½	8¼	8¼	...
51¾	39⅜	DukeP	2.80	6.3	10	781	45¾	44½	44½	— 1
103½	84⅞	Duke pf	8.20	9.5	...	z200	86	86	86	— ½
8¾	7	DukeRIn	.81e	11.2	...	22	7¼	7	7¼	+ ¼
1⅜	1	DukeRCa	...	...		48	1	1	1	...
71¼	49⅜	DunBd s	1.50	2.3	27	2539	68	65⅝	65⅝	— ¾
14⅜	11⅜	DuqLt	1.20	9.8	6	3652	12⅜	12	12¼	...
21½	17	Duq pf	1.87	10.8	...	z300	17⅜	17⅜	17⅜	— ⅛
22¼	18¼	Duq pf	2.00	10.7	...	z340	18⅝	18⅝	18⅝	— ⅛
24	20	Duq pfG	2.10	10.4	...	z60	20¼	20¼	20¼	+ ¼
24¼	20½	Duq prK	2.10	10.0	...	37	21	20⅝	21	— ⅛
26¾	21	Duq pr	2.31	10.5	...	z7810	22	21⅝	22	...
30	20	DynAm	.20	.8	32	101	24⅜	24¼	24⅜	— ⅛
25¼	13¼	Dyncrp	.31	1.3	18	1140	24¼	23	23¾	— ½

Bonds

Bonds are called *fixed income securities* because the issuer promises to pay a bond's owner a fixed amount of interest for a specific time period. You become a bondholder in one of two ways: as an individual investor (see below) or by buying shares in a mutual fund (see Chapter 6).

How to Read a Bond Certificate (page 50)

(1) Giant American Corporation is borrowing money from the investing public by issuing bonds.

(2) Amount of bond: The "principal" or "face value" of the bond is $5,000.

(3) Coupon rate: The annual interest per each $1,000 GAC promises to pay the bond owner for the life of the bond. The coupon rate is 8 percent.

(4) Due date: The maturity date. This is a twenty-year bond.

(5) Jacqueline Smith: The registered owner who has agreed to lend GAC $5,000. If she sells her bond, a new certificate will be issued with the new owner's name.

(6) The issuer promises to return the bond owner's principal when the bond matures.

(7) Interest payments: $200 will be sent twice a year to the registered owner of the bond.

(8) Call date: Some bonds may be redeemed or "called" before maturity. This bond cannot be redeemed for ten years.

(9) Transfer agent: Usually a bank, the transfer agent is responsible for sending interest payments to the bond owners and redeeming bonds at maturity.

A BOND CERTIFICATE

$5,000 (2)   GIANT AMERICAN CORPORATION (1) $5,000 (2)

8% (3) BOND DUE ON NOVEMBER 15, 2007 (4)

Giant American Corporation promises

to pay to

JACQUELINE SMITH (5)

the sum of   FIVE THOUSAND DOLLARS   DUE 2007

on November 15, 2007 (6) and to pay interest (7) at the rate of 8% semiannually on May 15 and November 15 each year until the principal is paid. This bond is subject to redemption prior to its stated maturity date on or after May 15, 1997. (8)

Giant American Corporation

DATED: November 15, 1987

PRESIDENT

FIRST NATIONAL BANK

Transfer Agent (9)

How To Read
The Bond-Market Page

Bonds are sold in $1,000 multiples, making $1,000 the "par," or original price, of a bond. If a bond's price subsequently falls *below par*, perhaps to $950, it is said to be selling at a *discount*. If it rises *above par*, perhaps to $1,050, it is selling at a *premium*.

When bond prices are quoted by a bond broker or in the newspaper, the last zero of the price is left off. Par becomes 100, the discount price is 95, and the premium price is 105.

The price for which you sell a bond might be the same as, more, or less than you paid for it.

Why Interest Rates and Bond Prices Change
(and One Goes Up When The Other Comes Down)

September 1, 1987: Giant American Corporation (GAC) issues $50 million bonds in $1,000 units with a twenty-year maturity. The *coupon rate* is 8%. This means that GAC promises to pay $80 per $1,000 each year for 20 years to whomever owns these bonds. The coupon rate is determined by such factors as the maturity of the bond, GAC's credit rating (see page 55) and the current *yield* on bonds of lesser, similar or higher quality.

The current yield of a bond is the relationship between its annual interest income and its current market price. If a GAC bond sells for $1,000 on September 1, its current yield is the same as its coupon rate: 8%.

$$\frac{\text{Coupon Rate}}{\text{Market Price}} = \text{Current Yield} \quad \frac{\$80}{\$1,000} = 8\%$$

The coupon rate remains the same throughout the life of the bond; however, bond prices and current yields will change, and change in an inverse relationship. As the bond's price goes up, the current yield falls, and vice versa.

October 1, 1987: Because of inflationary expectations, an increase in the supply of bonds, a decline in the demand for bonds, or some combination of these factors, the twenty-year bonds of National Electronics Corporation

(NEC) are issued to yield 8.5%. No prospective bond buyer will buy a GAC bond which pays $80 a year when she can buy an NEC bond that pays $85. Therefore, the GAC bond issued for $1,000 in September falls to $941 in October in order to yield the same interest rate as the NEC bond.

$$\frac{\text{Coupon Rate}}{\text{Market Price}} = \text{Current Yield} \quad \frac{\$80}{\$941} = 8.5\%$$

Those who bought GAC bonds on September 1 and continue to own them on October 1 are unaffected by the change in price and current yield unless they decide to sell. If they sell, they will have a loss of $59 per bond ($1,000 - $941).

March 1, 1988: Inflationary expectations have fallen, the supply of bonds has declined, and the demand for existing bonds has increased. The price of GAC bonds rises to $1,050, now producing a current yield of 7.6%.

$$\frac{\text{Coupon Rate}}{\text{Market Price}} = \text{Current Yield} \quad \frac{\$80}{\$1,050} = 7.6\%$$

If the original bondholders sell on March 1, they will have a capital *gain* of $50 per bond.

Although the coupon remains the same ($80) until the bond matures or is called, bond prices and yields fluctuate in an inverse relationship. When bond prices go up, yields fall, and vice versa.*

Who Issues Bonds?

The federal government issues the most creditworthy (lowest risk) bonds because they are backed by the U.S. Treasury and federal government agencies. Government bonds that mature within two to ten years are called *notes*. Minimum investment: $5,000 for two to three years, $1,000 for four years or longer (except for savings bonds).

*The simple calculation of current yield is used to illustrate the inverse relationship between bond prices and interest rates. In fact, the *yield to maturity* (the income earned by a bondholder until a bond matures) will be greater than the current yield if a bond is purchased at a discount, and lower than the current yield if a bond is purchased at a premium.

"Governments" with maturities longer than ten years are called *bonds*. Minimum investment: $1,000.

"Ginnie Mae" certificates, issued by the Government National Mortgage Association, represent a "package" of federally guaranteed mortgages. Certificate owners receive monthly payments of interest and principal. The government guarantees repayment of principal on the mortgages. *It does not guarantee a fixed interest rate.*

Ginnie Maes are issued with a maturity of twenty years, but annual income declines each year as mortgages are paid off and principal is returned to the investors. (See also GNMA mutual funds on page 62.)

"Flower" bonds are low-coupon (3 to 4.5%) Treasury bonds that may be purchased at a discount and used to pay federal estate taxes. Credit is given for the full face value of the bond. For example, $100,000 worth of flower bonds purchased for $80,000 will be accepted as full payment for a $100,000 estate tax bill.

Local and state government ("municipal") bonds are known as *tax-free* bonds because the interest earned is exempt from federal income tax, and exempt from state tax in the state of issue. However, if a municipal bond is sold before maturity at a higher price than its original purchase price, the *capital gain* is taxable.

The interest on some municipal bonds issued after August 15, 1986, is taxable. These are referred to as "private-purpose bonds" because funds raised are either passed on to non-government organizations or used for private activities, such as housing or health-care facilities.

Some municipal bonds are "insured." This means the bondholder will be paid off by a private insurance company if the issuer defaults. Insured bonds generally have higher credit ratings than non-insured bonds of comparable quality.

"Municipals" are issued for one to forty-year maturities. Minimum investment: $5,000.

Private corporation bonds, because they are a relatively higher risk than "governments" of comparable maturities, pay relatively higher yields.

Corporate bonds are issued with twenty-five to forty-year maturities. Minimum investment: $1,000.

Types of Bonds

Convertible bonds are corporate bonds that give an investor the option to exchange her bond for a specific number of shares of the company's common stock. "Convertibles" are purchased by investors who expect the common stock to rise. Their expected profit comes from the difference between the stock's selling price when they buy the convertible and its "conversion price." In the interim, they receive higher income in the form of interest payments as bondholders than they would have as shareholders.

Discount bonds are bonds selling at a lower price than the price when issued. Their current yield may be the same as new issues, but their coupon rate will be lower and its *total return* (also called *yield to maturity*) will be higher. For example, a discount bond with an $80 coupon and twenty years to maturity that sells for $850 has a yield to maturity of 9.5%. The new twenty-year bond selling for $1,000 with an $80 coupon has an 8% yield to maturity.

Zero coupon bonds (ZCBs) are bonds issued by the U.S. Treasury, corporations, or municipalities that are "stripped" of their coupons. No interest is paid out while you own the bond; the interest accumulates and becomes part of the principal when the certificates mature. Because individuals must pay taxes on the income they do not receive, taxable ZCBs are more appropriate for a tax-sheltered vehicle, like an Individual Retirement Account, than for direct ownership.

Registered and Bearer Bonds

All recently issued "governments," "corporates" and "municipals," are *registered* bonds. The owner's name and address is recorded with the bond issuer's transfer agent (U.S. Treasury for "governments"). The transfer agent sends interest payments to the registered owner twice a year.

Outstanding bonds may be either registered or *bearer* bonds. The latter literally belongs to "the bearer," the person who has possession. A bearer-bond owner does not receive interest checks in the mail. On each semiannual interest date, she must remove ("clip") a coupon that is attached to the side or bottom of her bond certificate. She deposits the coupon in her transaction account as if it were a check, and the bank forwards the coupon to the transfer agent for collection.

How To Compare Taxable With Tax-Free Yields

Use this formula:

$$\frac{\text{Tax-free Yield}}{(1 - \text{Your Tax Bracket})} = \text{Equivalent Taxable Yield}$$

Example

If a municipal bond is yielding 8% and you are in the 28% tax bracket, divide 8% by (1 — 0.28).

$$\frac{8\%}{(1-0.28)} = \text{Current Yield} \qquad \frac{\$8}{0.72} = 11.1\%$$

You would have to earn 11.1% on a U.S. government bond or corporate bond on which you pay *federal income tax* to earn the after-tax equivalent of 8%. If you pay state income taxes, the taxable equivalent is higher than 11.1%.

Choosing a High-Quality Bond

You should buy only municipal bonds and corporate bonds "rated" by Standard & Poor's or Moody's, two independent credit-rating agencies. Both agencies use a letter-rating system to indicate relative quality among issuers for financial stability and likelihood of making interest and principal payments to bondholders.

Standard & Poor's	Moody's
AAA	Aaa
AA	Aa
A	A
BBB	Baa
BB	Ba
B	B
CCC	Caa
CC	Ca
C	C
D	

The first four ratings in each system are considered "investment grade." Bonds become more speculative, and a higher risk to the investor, as their ratings descend.

All federal government securities are rated Triple A, making "governments" the highest quality and least risky fixed-income security.

Within each category from double A through B, Standard & Poor's uses a plus sign (+) to indicate relatively high quality and a minus sign (—) to indicate relatively low quality. Moody's uses numbers (1, 2 and 3).

Where to Buy Stocks and Bonds

The Federal Reserve Bank has twelve district offices and fifteen regional offices around the United States and sells only new Treasury bills, notes and bonds. There is no service charge, and you may pay by mail or in person. "The Fed" accepts personal checks. You can get information about new issues in advance of their sale dates from the business page of your newspaper or by calling a Fed office.

Full-service stockbrokers offer a wide variety of investment services: investment recommendations, research reports, safe-keeping of securities, money-market funds, even transaction accounts and credit cards. Full-service brokers are compensated by a commission or service charge on each security purchase or sale.

Discount brokers are brokerage houses whose only service is to place orders for security purchases and sales. They have no investment management, advisory or research services. They charge lower commissions than full service brokers for orders of the same size. Commissions on "odd lots," stock transactions of less than 100 shares, are higher than "round lot" transactions of 100 shares or more at both full service and discount brokers.

Customer securities departments at banks, like discount brokers, only buy and sell securities at their customers' direction. Banks offer investment information and investment management through their trust departments. Bank service charges and commissions may be more, less, or the same as full-service or discount brokers. *Shop around—stock and bond sales charges vary.*

Should You Hold Your Own Securities?

Stocks and bonds purchased by a customer but registered in the name of a brokerage firm and kept by the firm are said to be held in *street name.*
This is done for convenience by customers who travel a great deal, who do not want to keep track of dividend and interest payments, or who buy and sell securities frequently. It is required of those who purchase securities "on the margin" (see page 23).

Some brokerage houses try to encourage customers who do not fall in these categories to leave their securities in street name, ostensibly for safety and convenience. However, brokers may use securities held in street name as collateral for low-interest loans from banks. These funds become realtively low-cost working capital for a firm, or the source of loans to margin customers.

The primary drawback to leaving securities in street name is that all customer accounts are frozen if a brokerage house goes bankrupt. At best, securities held in street name will be distributed to their owners after a brief delay. If the securities cannot be returned, their current cash value is paid to investors by the Securities Investor Protection Corporation. The SIPC insures each customer's account against a maximum $500,000 loss, but it can take a year or longer for customers' claims to be filed and settled.

Unless you travel or trade a lot, keep your securities in a safe deposit box where you can get to them as needed.

TAKING STOCK OF STOCKS AND BONDS

6 The Feeling is Mutual

Mutual funds are investment companies which buy stocks and bonds issued by many corporations. Like money-market funds, the shares of a mutual fund are owned by a large number of investors. A mutual fund distributes the dividends and interest earned on the stocks and bonds it owns to the fund shareholders in proportion to the number of shares of the fund they own.

Why Buy Mutual Funds?

• A mutual fund can buy many more stocks and bonds than an individual with limited means. The more diversified a portfolio is, the more *diversified* the *risk*.

• *Professional management* is on the job every day. Experienced professionals whose only job is to keep your money safe and growing are likely to do a better job than someone who is not a full-time investment manager.

• Mutual funds permit investments of *small amounts* of money, as little as $25 initially, $10 to $100 subsequently.

• Stocks bought in large quantities are purchased at a *lower price* and *lower commissions* than most individuals pay.

• You can opt to have your *dividends reinvested* in additional shares and have more money working for you in the fund.

• You can opt for an *automatic investment plan* which transfers an amount you authorize out of your transactions account into your mutual fund each month.

- If your fund is one of a "family of funds" managed by the same investment company, you can authorize *exchanges*—sell $2,000 of the ABC fund to buy $2,000 of the XYZ fund—as your investment objectives change.

- You have *liquidity* with your mutual fund if you arrange to withdraw shares by writing a check (often for a $250 minimum) or have funds wired, upon telephone request, to your transaction account.

- You have *government protection* by stringent federal and state requirements, and by continual supervison of mutual funds by the Securities and Exchange Commission (SEC).

Load and No-Load Funds

If you buy a "load" fund, a sales charge, usually from 5% to 8.5% of your purchase, is deducted. If the fund is "front-loaded," the commission is deducted at the time of purchase. For example: You "invest" $1,000 but an 8% sales charge is taken out (the "load"). Therefore, only $920 is actually working for you.

"Back-loaded" funds invest the full amount they receive from investors, but impose a "termination" or "redemption" fee which gets lower the longer you hold the fund. For example: You invest $1,000. If you sell your shares at the end of one year in a fund with an 8% back load, you receive the current value of your shares plus accumulated income, less $80. At the end of three years, the redemption fee might be only 5%.

If you buy a "no-load" fund, there is no sales charge. The fund's management is compensated by a fee which is a percentage (0.5% to 1%) of the average daily value of the fund's net assets. The fee is deducted from income paid to shareholders. For example: You invest $1,000. The mutual fund earns 6%. The management fee is 0.5%. You receive a 5.5% dividend on $1,000.

Generally, stockbrokers sell "load funds" and fund organizers sell their own funds as "no loads," but some popular high-performance funds sold directly by their organizers charge a commission.

Open-End and Closed-End Funds

An "open-end" fund has no fixed amount of shares bought and sold by investors. It sells fund shares to new investors so long as there is a demand for them or until the fund itself has gotten so large it limits new shares to current shareholders.

The only buyer of an open-end fund's shares is the fund itself, which redeems at net asset value (NAV)—a fund's net worth divided by the number of outstanding shares on the day of redemption. Funds sold by large mutual-fund companies, such as Dreyfus, Fidelity and Vanguard, and *most* funds sold by brokers are open-end funds.

A "closed-end" fund is organized and sold with a specific number of shares. These shares are then "traded" between current buyers and prospective buyers, like common stock, with share prices set by "the market."

A "unit trust" is similar to a closed-end fund in that the trust is organized and sold with a fixed number of "units." However, unlike mutual funds, which are continually buying and selling stocks and bonds, the original investments in a unit trust—usually municipal bonds or other fixed income securities—are "frozen." The lack of flexibility in weeding out good investments turned bad makes a unit trust a riskier buy than a fixed-income mutual fund. Unit trusts are sold only by brokers and, like load funds, with a commission.

Different Funds for Different Objectives

For the highest income consistent with preservation of principal and liquidity, consider

Money-market funds, which are mutual funds which purchase large-denomination money-market instruments, such as Treasury bills and bank-issued certificates of deposit. The interest earned, which might be higher than the rates paid on savings accounts, is passed along to the shareholders. Money-market fund interest rates change as the yields on the securities in their portfolios change.

The minimum investment is as low as $500. There is no sales charge for putting money into or taking money out of your account. Share prices remain the same at all times. There is no minimum holding period. Money market funds are safe, but not as safe as insured savings instruments. They are liquid and relatively high yielding for short-term investments.

Tax-free money-market funds, which are made up of investments that earn interest exempt from federal and some state income taxes. The formula on Page 63 can tell you if your tax bracket warrants tax-free income. Money-market funds may be purchased directly from a fund's sponsor or through a stockbroker.

U.S. government money-market funds, which invest only in obli-gations of the U.S. Treasury and federal government agencies maturing in one year or less, are designed for investors who want a higher yield than an insured bank instrument, but not even the low risk of the non-insured private-sector securities held by "plain vanilla" money market funds.

*For the highest income consistent
with minimal fluctuations in principal, consider*

Short-term and intermediate-term bond funds, which invest in fixed- income securities with an average maturity that may be as short as four years or as long as ten. The longer the maturity, the greater the potential price volatility. Buy as "tax exempt" or "taxable," depending on your tax bracket.

*For the highest income currently available
but greatest potential price fluctuation, consider*

Investment-grade bond funds, which invest in corporate bonds or municipal bonds rated triple-B or better by Standard & Poor's or Moody's credit-rating agencies.

High-yield bond funds, which invest in corporate bonds or municipal bonds with lower credit ratings than "investment grade" bonds, indicating higher risk but also higher yields.

Insured municipal-bond funds, which invest in insured municipal bonds. They offer the assurance that if a bond issuer defaults, bondholders will receive interest and/or principal payments from a private insurance company such as American Municipal Bond Assurance Corporation (AMBAC) or Municipal Bond Insurance Association (MBIA).

State municipal-bond funds, which purchase only bonds issued by a state and the cities and municipal agencies in that particular state. The interest earned is exempt from state and local income taxes as well as federal for state residents.

"Ginnie Mae" funds, which purchase certificates issued by the Government National Mortgage Association. A Ginnie Mae fund shareholder, unlike an individual certificate holder, may request that principal repayments be reinvested in additional fund shares.

*For a total return that includes current income
and long-term growth potential, consider*

Growth and income funds, which purchase primarily high-quality common stocks and "convertibles" issued by companies whose stocks are expected to increase in value.

Convertible bond funds, which purchase bonds that can be exchanged for common stock expected to increase in value.

*For long-term growth with little or no
current income, consider*

Growth funds, which invest in common stocks and whose holdings range over the risk spectrum from conservative "blue chip" to highly speculative.

Some growth funds are *specialty funds*. They invest in stocks of a particular industry (e.g., financial services, health care), in stocks of foreign corporations or a particular foreign locale (e.g., Europe, Japan, Korea), in stocks of a particular end-product (e.g., gold or silver mines), or in stocks of "socially responsible" companies concerned not only with financial viability, but also with the effects of their products and corporate policies on employees, customers and other members of society.

How to Pick a Mutual Fund

What is your objective? Is it income? growth? income *and* growth? If it's income, shall it be taxable or tax free? You can select *several* mutual funds to meet different objectives.

Kay, a 65-year-old widow with $15,000 to invest, wants the highest income she can earn with minimal risk. She puts $5,000 in an investment-grade bond fund, $5,000 in a Ginnie Mae fund, and $5,000 in a high-yield bond fund.

Linda, who heads the marketing department of a major corporation, selects a growth fund for her retirement savings and a high-yield municipal-bond fund for tax-free current income.

Call or write for the prospectus of a fund that interests you. Most mutual funds have a toll-free telephone number. The fund's organizers are required to use the *prospectus* (from Latin for "to have looked forward") to inform prospective shareholders of the fund's investment objectives and policies, how shares may be purchased and redeemed, how the fund determines its share prices, dividend and capital-gains distribution policy, and expenses incurred by the fund, including management compensation.

For maximum flexibility if your investment objectives change, choose a fund that offers the no-charge option of switching your money to other funds managed by the same company.

Money magazine and *Barron's*, a weekly financial newspaper, periodically print tables of the best-performing income, growth, and growth-and-income funds.

Compare a fund's one-year, three-year and ten-year track record with comparable funds. As Damon Runyon said in another context, "The race is not always to the swiftest, nor the prize to the fairest, but all things considered, that's the way to bet."

Call the fund and ask for clarification of information you do not understand or cannot find in the prospectus. If the call-taker is patient, pleasant and helpful, that's a sign of a fund committed to good service. If the call-taker is rude, ill-informed or leaves you on "hold" for ten minutes with elevator music blaring in your ear . . . well, it's your nickel.

How to Buy a Mutual Fund

Directly from the fund

By mail: send in a completed application with a check for the amount of your initial investment. (Make certain it meets the fund's initial minimum investment requirement.)

By telephone: you will be assigned an account number to cite when you mail or wire funds.

In person: go to one of the offices that some mutual funds have opened in major cities (Boston, New York, Philadelphia, Chicago, Denver, Dallas, Los Angeles).

Through your stockbroker Most brokerage transactions are handled over the telephone; however, you may want to have a personal consultation with your broker to discuss his or her recommendations.

How to Keep Up With Your Mutual Fund

Some funds send out account statements every month; others, only four times a year. If you have a question in the interim, call the fund's shareholder services department or your stockbroker. Shareholders also receive periodic publications—annual reports, new prospectuses,etc.—which include current financial statements and lists of assets owned by the funds.

Daily newspapers publish the current NAV (net asset value) and "offer" price (what a prospective buyer is willing to pay) for hundreds of open-end funds in a mutual-funds table in their business sections. Prices, dividends and yields of closed-end funds may be found in the New York or American Stock Exchange tables or the over-the-counter (OTC) market listings.

Compare the current market value of your holding with your initial investment by multiplying the number of shares you own by the fund's current share price.

For example: In January, you bought 200 shares in the Rapid Growth Fund of America for $10 a share. By June the fund's current share price is $12. You have a "paper profit" of $400.

The number of shares now owned may be more than the number of shares purchased initially if you bought additional shares subsequently, or your income and capital gains are automatically reinvested.

How to Sell Shares in a Mutual Fund

By writing out a check, if the fund has issued you a checkbook. If you are closing out an account, call the fund for an up-to-date share price and number of shares you own.

By telephone request. If you sign up for telephone redemption, a fund will sell the required number of shares and usually mail a check within five business days. If you sign up for "expedited" redemption, a fund can wire your money the next business day to your designated transactions account.

By written request. A fund will redeem shares at the current net-asset value on the day the request is received and usually mail a check within seven business days. The fund will require the return of any share certificates issued to you and may require that your signature be "guaranteed" by an officer of a commercial bank.

For further information about mutual funds, write to

> No Load Mutual Fund Association
> 11 Penn Plaza
> Suite 2204
> New York NY 10117
>
> Investment Company Institute
> 1775 K Street NW
> Washington DC 20006

7 There's No Place Like Home

Can you afford to buy a house or condominium? One rule of thumb: One month's housing expense should be no more than 28% of your monthly pre-tax income. Another guideline used by mortgage lenders: Total debt including mortgage payments should be no more than 36% of your pre-tax income.

Home ownership is a top-priority financial goal for many people. To see if you can afford to buy a house, obtain the information you need from a mortgage lender and the homeowner whose house you want to buy. Then fill in the following form. (b) should not exceed (a).

Monthly income before taxes	$_____
times 28% equals	
Monthly affordable housing expenditure	$_____ (a)
Purchase price of house	$_____
less	
Down payment	$_____
equals	
Mortgage	$_____
One month's mortgage payment	$_____
plus	
1/12 annual real estate taxes	$_____
plus	
1/12 annual homeowner's insurance premium	$_____
equals	
Total monthly housing expense	$_____ (b)

> *Lenders are required to take all sources of income into account in determining a prospective home buyer's creditworthiness (see page 24.)*

How to Buy a House

Before you become a serious buyer, identify the area you like and go "window shopping" at open houses on weekends. This will give you an idea of relative values in the neighborhood. If you are working with a real estate agent, she will set up appointments for you.

Offer When you find a house you want to be your home, make a written offer to the seller which includes the price you are willing to pay and a deadline for the seller's response. An *earnest money* deposit of $500 to $1,000 is usually required as evidence of the purchaser's sincerity.

If your offer is accepted, you will sign a *purchase and sale agreement* which sets the *closing date*—when you will take possession of the property—and other terms of the sale. An additional deposit is required which usually brings the *down payment* to 5% or 10% of the purchase price.

Interest If you are represented by an agent, your deposit will be held in an *escrow* account until it is transferred to the seller at *settlement*, the closing date. **Request an interest-earning escrow account.** Sometimes the buyer gets 100% of the income earned, sometimes you divide it with the seller.

Contingency Make certain your agreement has a mortgage-contingency clause that says you are released from your obligation and get back your deposit if you cannot obtain a mortgage within a specific period of time. The clause should include the maximum mortgage rate you are willing to pay.

Mortage rates change continually. The 9% that was quoted last Monday could be 9.25% on Tuesday and 9.5% next Monday. Also, lenders' policies differ on locking in the rate in effect on the day you appear to fill in an application. One lender might make a firm commitment to that rate for as long as it takes to have your application approved. Another's commitment might hold for a specific time period, such as ninety days. Still another might be willing to give you a lower rate if mortgage rates drop during the time you wait for approval but not increase your rate if mortgage rates rise.

At settlement, your money—the *down payment*—and the funds you've borrowed from the mortgage lender are transferred to the seller. The buyer also must pay *closing costs*. These expenses include a new property deed and *title insurance*, the assurance that the seller has clear title to, and therefore the right to sell, the property.

Property taxes are usually collected two or four times a year. Pay the taxes yourself when they come due rather than combining tax payments with your monthly mortgage payment to the mortgage holder. With the latter arrangement, you are making an interest-free loan to the mortgage company before it has to transfer your money to the local taxing authority. If you are making monthly tax payments with an existing mortgage, request an interest-earning escrow account for the money set aside until the tax bill is due.

Have a lawyer, ideally one who specializes in real estate, review all documents you are asked to sign relating to the purchase of your new home. The lawyer's fee is a worthwhile expense for protecting your interest and providing peace of mind. It also may be a tax-deductible expense if you itemize deductions on your tax return for that year.

**Where to Go
for a Mortgage**

• First choice: A financial institution from which you have received a mortgage or a loan in the past.

• Savings and Loan associations (also known as "Building and Loans").

• Savings banks. Commercial banks. Credit unions. Mortgage companies.

• Realtors who can introduce you to financial institutions they work with on a regular basis.

• Builders of new residences who have commitments for mortgage money from institutional lenders.

• The present owner of the house or apartment you wish to buy.

Kinds of Home Financing

Fixed-rate mortgages A fixed-rate mortgage is the traditional home mortgage on which you make equal monthly payments of principal and interest over the life of the loan.

If you have a choice between a fifteen-year mortgage and a thirty-year mortgage at the same rate, your *monthly* payment will be higher on the fifteen-year payout. However, *total* payments are higher on the thirty-year mortgage, and equity builds up at a slower rate.

In addition to the monthly interest charged on a loan, mortgage lenders charge a fee in the form of "points" on new mortgage applications. Each "point" is equal to one percent of the mortgage. For example, if you are charged three points on a $60,000 mortgage, you pay $1,800 to the lender, perhaps one point with your mortgage application and the other two points at closing.

If you have a choice between paying more points (e.g., three rather than two) in order to get a lower annual interest rate (e.g., 10% rather than 10.25%), consider the time period over which you think you'll own the property. The further out your time horizon, the greater the advantage of the higher points and lower mortgage rate combination because the expense of the "points" is spread out over a relatively longer period of time. Points, like interest payments, are deductible expenses on your federal tax return.

Adjustable-rate mortage The interest rate on an ARM is usually fixed for the first six months or one year; subsequently, it is "adjusted" up or down every six or twelve months as currently prevailing interest rates move up or down. There is a limit on how much an interest rate can be raised or lowered from one "adjustment period" to the next. Lenders are required to set a cap on the highest rate that may be charged during the life of the mortgage and may place a floor under the lowest rate.

Assumable mortgage When a seller has the right to transfer her low-interest mortgage to a buyer, the mortgage is said to be "assumable." It might not be assumable if the mortgage includes a clause which says the lender has the right to full payment of the outstanding balance if a property is sold.

Graduated-payment mortgage The monthly payment is smaller during the early years of the mortgage and larger during the later years.

Balloon mortgage A variation of the graduated payment mortgage, a "balloon" mortgage holder makes relatively small monthly payments, perhaps interest only, for five or ten years and one large, or"balloon," payment when the mortgage is terminated.

Purchase-money mortgage The home seller holds the mortgage of her property's new owners. She might want to earn higher income than she could receive on more marketable fixed income securities, such as savings certificates and government bonds, and so might provide the mortgage at a lower interest rate than institutional lenders are offering.

Renegotiable-rate mortgage A variation of the adjustable rate mortgage. The interest rate is fixed for the first one to five years, then renegotiated subsequently for three- or five-year periods over the life of the mortgage.

Reverse annuity mortgage An arrangement designed for older people who wish to convert the equity in their mortgage-free homes into a source of income. It is a "reverse" mortgage because the homeowner builds up, rather than pays down, a debt obligation to the lender. It is an "annuity" because the homeowner can depend on a steady stream of income for five, ten or twenty years.

Shared-appreciation mortgage A mortgage given at a lower rate than currently prevailing interest rates. In return, the homeowner must share with the lender a specified proportion of any increase in the mortgaged property's value when it is sold.

Wraparound mortgage When interest rates are high, a home owner may offer this variation of the purchase money mortgage as an inducement to a prospective buyer. The seller's old, relatively low-rate mortgage is "wrapped" around a loan made from the seller to the buyer at a somewhat higher rate. The new owner makes amortized monthly payments to the former owner equal to the mortgage payment and the loan payment. The former owner passes along the payment on the first mortgage to the mortgage holder. Wraparounds usually are temporary arrangements until the new owner obtains permanent financing. The wraparound agreement should be drawn up by the original owner's lawyer.

Equity financing This permits a parent—or nonrelative—to receive tax advantages from a house being purchased by a new home buyer in return for a contribution to the down payment. The equity share received by the investor-owner does not have to be the same as the share of the down payment she provides, but the resident-owner is required to pay a fair market rental to the investor-owner in proportion to her equity share.

If the non-resident has a 50% equity share, and monthly rent for a comparable property is $600, the resident pays her $300 a month. Both investor-owners and resident-owners may deduct on their tax returns a *pro rata* share of the real-estate taxes and mortgage interest they pay. Investor-owners also are permitted to deduct their share of depreciation, repairs and maintenance. When the property is sold, owners share the profits (or loss) in proportion to their equity interests.

Swing or bridge loan When Home Buyer A has to close on her new house before she settles on her current residence with Home Buyer B, she might have to borrow an amount equal to the down payment on her new home. The collateral for the short-term loan is the property Home Buyer A is selling.

Should You Refinance Your Existing Mortgage?

Yes, if you stay in your home for the length of time it takes the sum of new mortgage payments and settlement charges to become less than the sum of current monthly payments. The closer your break-even point, the more advantageous the refinancing.

Before refinancing a new mortgage, try to renegotiate a *lower* interest rate on your existing mortgage with the present lender. You save the cost of a new title search, appraisal, recording fee, etc. The lender holds on to a good customer it might otherwise lose to a lower-rate lender.

If you refinance, remember: Points on a refinanced mortgage are usually amortized over the life of the loan. They are a tax-deductible expense in the year they are incurred only if the proceeds of the refinancing are used for additions or renovations to the property.

Secondary Financing

Second mortgages are made by homeowners who wish to borrow the "equity" in their residences that exceeds the amount of their first mortgage. Second mortgages are made at higher interest rates than first mortgages because the holder of a second mortgage has a legal right to payment from a defaulting borrower only after the first mortgage holder is paid off.

Home-equity loans differ from second mortgages mainly in that the loan proceeds of a second mortgage are received in one lump sum, while a home equity loan may be drawn down by check or credit card in the amount you need when you need it. Another distinction is that the interest rate on a second mortgage might be fixed or variable, while the interest rate on a home equity loan is almost always variable.

Borrowers pay settlement or closing costs on both second mortgages and home-equity loans. Costs include a title search, property appraisal, lien recording and "points."

8 Real Life Monopoly: The Real Estate Investment Game

Q. What are the three characteristics of a good real estate investment?
A. Location, location and location.

If any investment is a woman's investment, it seems to be real estate. We respond with a practiced eye to the features in a house or apartment that make it a desirable place to live. We mentally redecorate the pea-green-wallpapered eyesore. We know instinctively that a fresh coat of paint and new fixtures will do wonders for a thirty-year-old bathroom. And more than one real-estate entrepreneur got her start driving around town while the kids were in school, checking out and comparing good buys.

> When Mary and David decided to buy a house, Mary found a big old Victorian that had been divided into a two-family residence. A part of its appeal for her was that they could live on the first two floors, and use the rent from the third floor apartment to cover the mortgage. Also, the house was in a transitional suburban neighborhood close to the city. Mary concluded that other young couples who could not afford expensive new housing would be attracted by the spaciousness of the old properties, their gingerbread charm and the wide, tree-shaded streets.
>
> Concerned about the prospect of costly alterations, Mary and David bought the house only after being assured by a real estate appraiser that the property was structurally sound. They were able to keep their expenses down by doing painting and other cosmetic repairs themselves. Each year they hired a professional contractor for one large renovation project, such as a new kitchen or restoration of the splendid oak parquet floors. They had no trouble finding a tenant, and as Mary had predicted, the house turned out to be an excellent investment. They enjoyed all the tax advantages of being landlords while they lived there, and sold the house after five years for twice the price they'd paid for it.

Why Buy Real Estate?

As an inflation hedge While the Consumer Price Index rose an average of 7.2% per year between 1975 and 1985, the value of a single-family home rose an average of 12%.

For tax advantages Deductible expenses from federal income tax include:
Local real estate taxes.
Interest on mortgage payments.
Management and maintenance expenses.
Depreciation (the dollar amount a property is assumed to depreciate, or "wear out," each year).

For leverage Leverage is using borrowed funds on which you pay a fixed rate of interest to buy a property which you expect to increase in value. Here is a simplified example:

		$60,000 property
	less	$10,000 down payment
		$50,000 mortgage

Property sold in five years for	$100,000
less balance due on mortgage	$ 40,000
Return on $10,000 down payment	$ 60,000
(*less* five years of mortgage payments).	

For rental income Real estate is also bought to produce income, by renting it. The rule of thumb used to be that you only bought rental properties that produced *net* rental income (after expenses) of at least 10% of the property's purchase price. High real-estate prices and high mortgage rates have made 10% a difficult target to hit.

Most people therefore buy property today for the capital appreciation and tax benefits. However, it is possible for rental properties to become a good source of current income if annual rents go up faster than the rate of increase of expenses (taxes, maintenance, etc.)

Choosing a Location for a Real-Estate Investment

Best bet for the novice investor: A single home, a two-unit dwelling or a condominium in your own geographic area. Buying far from home in a "hot" real-estate market is tempting but unwise for the small investor unless you have some one there to look out for your interests. Professional real-estate managers charge 10 to 15% of gross rental income for their services.

Buy in a community where the demand for rental housing is rising faster than the supply.

Look for a region that's prosperous and expanding, or an inner-city neighborhood being rehabilitated. An older property might qualify for a one-time tax credit of 10% or 20% of renovation costs.

Things to Think About Before You Buy

• Real estate is an illiquid investment. It is not easily or quickly converted to cash.

• The price at which you might have to sell could be lower than the price you paid. If you lose money on a real-estate investment, will it affect your standard of living?

• If you don't have a tenant, can you afford to make monthly payments and maintain the property?

• Are you willing to take on the responsibilities of being a landlady: renting the property, maintaining and supervising the property, dealing with tenants' needs and complaints?

• Are you willing to incur the expense of hiring a manager to maintain your property and shield you from late-night calls from tenants?

THE REAL ESTATE INVESTMENT GAME

CALCULATING RETURN ON A REAL-ESTATE INVESTMENT

FIRST LIST THE FOLLOWING:

Expected Rental Income $ _____

One-Time Costs
    Property purchase price $ _____
        less
    Down payment $ _____
        equals
    Amount to be financed $ _____

    Estimated settlement costs $ _____
        (title insurance, property appraisal, points,
        recording & closing fees, legal fees, etc.)
    Renovation budget $ _____

Obtainable Mortgage Terms

      ____% plus ____ points for ____ years

On-going Costs
    Annual mortgage payments $ _____
    Annual real estate taxes $ _____
    Annual property and liability insurance $ _____
    Annual maintenance $ _____
    Annual management fees $ _____

Annual Depreciation $ _____
    (Divide 95% of the purchase price
    by 27.5 years for residential property
    and by 31.5 years for nonresidential property.)

Tax Credit $ _____
    (One-time 20% tax credit for rehabilitation
    expenses on a certified historic structure;
    one-time 10% tax credit on a *nonresidential*
    building built before 1936.)

THEN ESTIMATE:

Annual Cash Flow

    Rental income $ _____
        less
    mortgage payments $ _____
    other expenses $ _____
        equals
    Net Income $ _____

Annual Taxable Income

    Rental income $ _____
        less
    mortgage interest $ _____
    other expenses $ _____
    depreciation $ _____
        equals
    Taxable Income (or Loss) $ _____
    (See page 131 for discussion of limits
    on deductible losses.)

Annual Total Return

    Rental income $ _____
        less
    mortgage payments $ _____
    other expenses $ _____
        equals
    Net income $ _____
        plus
    Appreciation in property's value
        since previous year $ _____
        equals
    Total Return $ _____

If You Lack the Means or Experience to Do It Yourself

Start a real-estate investment club* Get together a group of friends. Decide how much each woman should contribute. (To keep business decisions manageable and investable funds realistic, there probably should be no more than ten members and a minimum initial contribution from each of at least $1,000.)

Have a partnership agreement prepared by an attorney. The agreement should state explicitly how to deal with such matters as cash deficits, unanticipated repairs, the death or incapacity of a partner, and all other situations the partnership might confront.

Ask a real-estate broker to advise your group and help you look for a purchase.

Invest in a real-estate investment trust (REIT) A REIT is a mutual fund that buys large real estate properties (apartment houses, office buildings, shopping centers), makes loans to developers of large-scale real estate projects, or does both. Rental income and mortgage payments are distributed as dividends to the shareholders. Proceeds of property sales are distributed as capital gains.

REITs are purchased by investors interested in current income and long-term capital appreciation. They offer the small investor the advantages of professional management, liquidity, diversification of risk and a real estate investment for a smaller amount of money than direct ownership would require. On the other hand, a REIT can be a high risk, low yield investment if vacancy rates are high and rental income is low relative to on-going operating and mortgage costs.

The best REIT is one that owns occupied rental properties and is run by experienced management.

---

* I first learned of the idea of women pooling their resources to buy real estate when Louise Gilbert, a suburban Philadelphia realtor, organized an investment club called *Femmes Seules* (Women Only) in 1974.

9 All That Glitters: Silver and Gold

People buy silver and gold for capital appreciation, protection against inflation, and insurance against "doomsday."

Karen thinks the demand for gold for ornamental and industrial uses will increase at a faster rate than the output of the world's gold mines will increase. She bought gold at $425 an ounce in 1986, and expects the price to be substantially higher when she sells it.

Recalling the double-digit price increases of the late 1970s and early 1980s, Bess believes she can better maintain the future purchasing power of her investment dollars with an asset like silver that has "intrinsic" (real) value than with assets denominated in depreciating dollars such as savings instruments, stocks and bonds. Although stocks and bonds pay dividends and interest, and Bess earns no income on the silver coins she's bought, she expects the appreciated value of her real assets to more than make up for the loss of income she could earn on "paper" assets.

Vera is alarmed by the never-ending succession of international crises emanating from all parts of the globe: terrorism, civil insurrection, military coups, territorial conflicts and man-made disasters that range from famine to malfunctioning nuclear power plants. She fears that a major economic or political catastrophe in the future will make paper money worthless. She buys gold coins as her "insurance policy" for such a time when only precious metals have value as a medium of exchange.

You Should Buy Silver or Gold Only If

• You can afford to lose all or part of your investment if you have to sell at a price lower than the price at which you bought.

• You have a substantial portfolio of income-producing assets.

• You are, or intend to become, a diligent, knowledgeable collector of numismatic coins.

How to Buy Silver and Gold

Bullion is a quantity designation for troy-ounce gold and troy-ounce silver. Gold and silver bullion are sold as gold bullion coins weighing 1/10 ounce to 1.2 ounces, gold bullion "wafers" weighing 1/20 ounce to one ounce, gold bullion bars weighing one ounce to 400 ounces, or silver bullion bars weighing one ounce to 1,000 ounces.

Prices reported in the newspapers and on daily radio and TV broadcasts are the New York Commodity Exchange (COMEX) prices for 100-ounce gold bars and 1,000-ounce silver bars. The price per ounce is higher for smaller quantities.

Gold bullion coins available for investment include the American Eagle, Austrian Corona and Ducat, British Sovereign, Canadian Maple Leaf, Dutch Ducat, Hungarian Corona and Ducat, Mexican Peso, and South African Krugerrand.

Silver bullion coins available include pre-1965 U.S. nickles, dimes, quarters, half-dollars and dollars (sold in "bags" of $1,000 face value).

Dealers sell bullion coins at a higher price ("premium") than the daily quoted bullion price.

Numismatic coins (collectors' coins) are priced according to age, rarity, historic interest and artistic quality as well as *intrinsic* value (i.e., metallic content per coin).

Commemorative coins or medallions are coins minted as collectors' items rather than as currency. Since 1980, the U.S. Treasury has issued half-ounce and one ounce gold medallions. The price of a medallion is based on the prevailing market value of its gold content plus the costs of manufacture and distribution.

Jewelry, such as a silver bracelet or an engraved gold disk memorializing the Statue of Liberty, are lovely to look at but much less desirable as investments than bullion and rare coins. You pay a mark-up over the value of the metal content for workmanship and the dealer's profit, and you'll sell an item you bought at retail price for its wholesale price.

Common stocks Shares in silver-and gold-mining companies may be bought for the prospect of capital appreciation *and* dividends. The value of a mine's shares depend on market price, the mine's output and potential, the quality of mine management, and the political environment (e.g., a political crisis in South Africa could have a major effect on world gold production).

Mutual funds Investment companies that hold shares in silver- and gold-mining companies operate on the same principles as the mutual funds described in Chapter 6.

Gold deposit receipts or certificates This is a mutual-fund concept. The organizing company buys a large quantity of gold. Participants are able to buy smaller quantities at a lower price than if they were making the purchases themselves. Certificates are issued to verify ownership. There is a minimum initial investment of $5,000 to $25,000, and an annual maintenance fee. A company may guarantee repurchase of its units at a specified premium over the current market price.

Where to Buy Silver and Gold

- Commercial banks.
- Stockbrokers.
- Currency dealers.
- Mutual-fund organizations.
- Precious-metal dealers.
- Coin-dealer "exchanges."
- Jewelers.

Remember

- You earn no interest on bullion or coins.

- The smaller the unit, the higher the price when buying and the lower the price when selling.

- In addition to the purchase price, you pay a transactions fee (premium, commission or sales charge) and sales tax.

- You may have to pay shipping or storage charges.

- For security, silver and gold purchases should be kept in a safe deposit box and be insured.

- You will pay an assay fee (evaluation of metal's quality) when you sell.

Request a written guarantee of your purchase's "fineness" (the proportion or amount of pure metal it contains).

- Comparison shop—prices, premiums and other charges vary.

10 Delectable Collectibles

"Collectibles" is a grab-bag word created to describe such assets as fine art, antiques, precious gems, stamps, coins and old books purchased because they are expected to increase in value.

There have always been *collectors* who buy works of art for their beauty and quality, *antiquers* who haunt estate sales and junk shops, and *hobbyists* for whom the satisfaction of knowing why a rare stamp or coin is rare is as important as the acquisition itself. It is only in recent years that the combination of widespread affluence, double-digit inflation and high taxes has motivated large numbers of people to invest in collectibles. Simultaneously, and in the true spirit of American enterprise, a large number of "investment opportunities" has been created to meet every taste and pocketbook.

However, access to profitable collectible investing is not quite as egalitarian as vendors of collectibles would have us believe. Most of the people who have the time, money and expertise to make a killing in fine art, precious gems and coin collecting are professional dealers, tenacious hobbyists or are already wealthy.

Novice investors of modest means usually are better off concentrating on antique or classic furniture, *objects d'art* (everything from ceramic thimbles to leaded glass windows), old books, and items that evoke curiosity or nostalgia for a historic period. These are the finds that still turn up in thrift shops and musty old bookstores, at flea markets and yard sales. (The pros and the rich are out there too, but on a more equal footing. In scavenging, the race is to the swift.)

These kinds of collectibles offer a particularly fertile field for women. Many are everyday household items that homemakers are familiar with. A woman who enjoys bargain-hunting can learn to recognize a Queen Anne chair leg as easily as she recognizes a designer dress in Filene's Basement. At night she can read *Antiques* magazine as well as *Better Homes and Gardens*. She and her friends can substitute no-calorie auction forays for weekday luncheons.

Successful collectible investors need not love the things they buy. They do need to be knowledgeable, persistent and lucky.

When You Buy Collectibles

All good collectible investments have four characteristics:

• They are perceived to be the highest quality by experts in the field.

• They are unique or in short supply relative to the demand for them.

• They cannot be converted into cash quickly and easily.

• They have high market risk. Relative to other investments, there is a high probability that the price at which they are sold will be lower than the price at which they were purchased.

If you buy retail, choose a dealer who is well known in your community, recommended by someone whose opinion you value, and/or is a member of one of the following organizations:

Art: Art Dealers' Association of America
Antiques: National Association of Antique Dealers
Coins: Professional Numismatic Guild
Stamps: American Stamp Dealers' Association

Get a *written* description of your purchase and a guarantee of the item's authenticity from the seller. (Auction houses usually do not verify the authenticity of the collectibles they sell.) *Save* your sales receipt or cancelled check. Verification of the date of purchase and the purchase price might be needed in the future.

Do Not Purchase Collectibles Blindly Through The Mail

When you see a tempting newspaper, magazine or mail-order advertisement for collectibles, write and ask the seller for local references. Know *exactly* what you are getting *before* you pay for it. ("Investment-grade emeralds for $100 from South America" could be ten microscopic chips with no resale value.) Make certain there are no strings attached to a "money-back guarantee."

---

84   THE NEW MONEY WORKBOOK FOR WOMEN

What Are Your Collectibles Worth?

A collection should be inventoried and appraised periodically. This is useful for tax purposes if the collector sells an item or dies, and for insurance claims if an item is lost or stolen.

Appraisals are done for a fee, and should be done by a qualified, reputable dealer who is a member of the American Society of Appraisers. The usual valuation standard is the most recent sale price of a comparable item.

Attach photographs to your inventory. Precise identification may aid recovery if possessions are lost or stolen.

COLLECTIBLES INVENTORY

_____ (date)

Description	Date	Amount	Value
_____	_____	_____	_____
_____	_____	_____	_____
_____	_____	_____	_____
_____	_____	_____	_____
_____	_____	_____	_____
_____	_____	_____	_____
_____	_____	_____	_____
_____	_____	_____	_____
_____	_____	_____	_____
_____	_____	_____	_____
_____	_____	_____	_____
_____	_____	_____	_____
_____	_____	_____	_____
_____	_____	_____	_____
_____	_____	_____	_____

When You Sell Collectibles

How to Sell
- Through print advertising.
- At a house sale.
- At a flea market.
- Through a dealer.
- On consignment at an auction.

Remember
- Quick resale profits on collectibles are unlikely. They usually must be held at least three to five years for sufficient price appreciation to warrant the investment.

- Taxes are paid on collectibles only when they are sold at a profit. There are no taxes due on "paper" gains (increases in value while you own an asset).

- If you buy retail, you sell wholesale. For example, the limited-edition print you bought in 1982 for $200 is selling in 1987 for $400. You decide to sell your print back to the gallery. Its buying price is $200, just about the amount the artist receives before the gallery's mark-up.

Tax Tips for Collectibles Investors

- The costs of appraising, insuring, mailing, storing and restoring collectibles may be deductible expenses for the collectible investor (i.e., she who collects primarily to make a profit).

- If a collectible item is exchanged for another collectible item of like kind, no tax is due on the appreciated value of the first item. However, the tax obligation is not entirely eliminated. It is deferred until the second item is sold.

- If a collector gives a work of art that has increased in value to a nonprofit institution (e.g., museum, favorite charity, college alumnae association), she may deduct part or all of the appreciated value of the gift from her taxable income if the recipient "uses the gift as part of its regular business." If the organization sells the art work, the donor's deduction may not exceed her original cost.

• A collector who makes gifts from her collection will not have those collectibles included in her taxable estate when she dies *if* she does not retain a "present interest" in the gift. This means that the recipient must have immediate *possession* and *control* of the stamp collection, the Chippendale desk, Picasso plate, or whatever during the donor's lifetime.

• The value of charitable contributions that exceed $5,000 must be verified with a recent evaluation by a professional appraiser in order to qualify for a tax deduction.

11 A Tax Shelter is Not a Home

The best tax shelter is an economically sound investment.
Tax savings are just the frosting on the cake.

It's easy to understand why someone like Harold, a dentist who wants to give up his practice and retire to Florida, is attracted by such prospects as a "20% historic rehab credit" and "100% first-year write-offs." The problem is that Harold hasn't the faintest notion how rehab credits and write-offs will contribute to the income he needs in order to retire. His wife Doris decides she had better find out.

What Doris learns is that any investment that offers the opprtunity to reduce, defer or eliminate income taxes is a tax shelter. Municipal bonds "shelter" the income they pay (Chapter 5). So do real-estate investments (Chapter 8) and government-regulated retirement plans (Chapter 12).

The phrase *tax shelter* is used most frequently to describe certain kinds of large-scale projects in which participations are sold as *limited partnerships*. Economic activities organized as partnerships include real estate development, oil and gas drilling, farming, cattle breeding, timber raising and mineral excavation.

Until recently, the federal government offered preferential tax treatment to all investors in these activities because they are considered relatively high risk and important for the country's economic welfare. If the projects were successful, investors were rewarded with higher after-tax income than they might expect to earn from other investments.

Because of changes in the tax law, as of January 1, 1987, only individuals who actively participate in such business ventures may derive preferential tax benefits, and even these benefits have been scaled down.

How Limited Partnerships Work

The partners in a limited partnership are *investors*. They have no responsibility for or involvement in day-to-day administration and operations. It is a *limited* partnership because each partner's liability for the debts of the organization is limited to the amount she has invested.

The organizer of a limited partnership is the *general partner*. The general partner may be one or more people or a corporation. The general partner receives a management fee and shares in income earned by the partnership. The general partner may or may not have invested in the partnership.

Profits earned and losses incurred by the partnership are distributed in proportion to the ownership shares of each investor. The cost of a partnership participation ranges from $1,000 a share to $100,000 or more.

Partnership interests are sold directly by the organizers and/or through stock-brokerage firms and other vendors of financial products who earn a commission on each share they sell. The best shelters are private partnerships which successful entrepreneurs organize and offer to a small group of their friends and business associates.

If you were a limited partner in a shelter before 1987, you

• were able to deduct losses from all your taxable income up to the amount you were *at risk*; that is, the sum of money initially invested in a project plus any funds borrowed by the partnership for which you were personally liable. (Investors in real-estate shelters were exempt from the at-risk rule.)

• paid a lower tax when the partnership sold an appreciated asset owned for more than a year than you would pay on the same amount of salary or investment income.

If you are a limited partner in a tax shelter after 1986, you will

• have income earned from the partnership classified as *passive* income if you are not an active participant in the partnership's business activities.

A TAX SHELTER IS NOT A HOME

• be able to use passive losses from the shelter *only* as an offset to income *earned from other tax shelters during the same year*. ("Excess" losses may be carried forward to offset passive income earned in future years.)

• be subject to the at-risk rules as a real estate investor.

• derive lower tax benefits from investments undertaken with the assumption that you would be in a tax bracket of 40% or higher. The highest tax rate is 38.5% for 1987 and 28% after 1987.

• have fewer deductible losses. An extended depreciation schedule on buildings and equipment provides for smaller write-offs each year and the real estate tax credit has been cut back. (Interest payments on partnership debts remain deductible but have less value as an offset to income for an investor in the 28% bracket than an investor who was in the 50% bracket.)

• pay the *same* tax when the partnership sells an appreciated asset as you would pay on the same amount of salary or investment income.

• be permitted to deduct all losses *only* when you sell your entire interest in the tax shelter.

• Partners in shelters in operation before 1987 will be permitted to deduct from other income 65% of excess losses in 1987, 40% in 1988, 20% in 1989 and 10% in 1990.

Should You Dispose of Your Tax Shelter?

If your investment no longer seems to offer the long-term growth prospects it had when you purchased it, and you no longer are able to reduce current taxable income with substantial deductions from tax shelter losses, you may be thinking about selling your partnership interest. Selling is more easily said than done.

There is no organized market, such as the New York Stock Exchange, for the purchase and sale of limited partnership shares. Some partnership agreements offer the possibility—rarely the promise—that a limited partner's shares will be acquired by the general partner. If it is, the buy-back price is likely to be far below the original cost of the partnership interest. The only alternative to the general partnership is likely to be a "shelter exchange" which, for a fee comparable to a brokerage commission, makes a market between buyers and sellers of partnerships.

The good news associated with selling a partnership interest before the partnership itself terminates is that you are permitted to deduct all accumulated passive losses against passive *or* non-passive income. The bad news is that past tax deductions taken for "accelerated depreciation" are recaptured. The result can be a high capital-gains tax on the difference between the amount you receive when you sell and an "adjusted cost basis" on the amount you actually paid even if the partnership interest is sold at a loss.

Limited partners committed to making future payments of as much as $10,000 a year to a partnership with bleak economic prospects and low sheltering value must wrestle with the dilemma of whether to cut their losses now or throw good money after bad. Defaulting on the outstanding debt is not a viable option for anyone who values a good credit standing. There also is the not-so-minor legal obligation to comply with a contractual agreement.

Under these circumstances, the relatively fortunate limited partners are those associated with a general partner who, for whatever reason, is willing to close down the partnership. Less fortunate limited partners must be more resourceful. They need to organize. Perhaps the general partner will take over their interest payments or pay off an existing mortgage. Perhaps the institutional lender will give the partnership a lower borrowing rate or even a grace period during which loan payments are suspended.

Is There a Good Post-1987 Tax Shelter?

A new kind of tax shelter, the "income partnership," has been created to generate, as the name implies, income. But not just any kind of income. This is *passive income* that can be offset by the passive losses from previously owned partnerships. Or, put another way, income from such sources as real-estate rentals and equipment-leasing contracts starts out as taxable and ends up as nontaxable because of deductible losses from the old partnership.

If you are considering an income partnership

• don't sign anything until a financial professional other than the seller of the partnership reviews the prospectus.

• ask to have terms you don't understand explained to you in plain English.

• know that an investment in a partnership is riskier than buying a corporate bond. Real-estate projects go bust as well as boom, and business-equipment technology is constantly changing. The income figures you see are projections, not guarantees.

• know that the income projections include a return of principal; that is, a partial payback of your original investment is included in each income check you receive.

• take time to add up the sales commissions, acquisition fees and organizational expenses of the partnership. These expenses might absorb as much as twenty cents out of each dollar you pay into the partnership.

• look for a general partner who has experience and a good track record in the partnership's line of business, not someone who hung out his shingle before the ink on the new tax bill was dry.

• compare the estimated return projected by the partnership with the return you might earn on other investments.

> *Don't buy anything from anybody who uses high-pressure tactics. There are few investments so "hot" that they require an instant decision, but there are many impulsive financial decisions investors have lived to regret.*

12 How to Enjoy Life After a Working Life

From birth to 18, a girl needs good parents. From 18 to 35, she needs good looks; from 35 to 55, a good personality. After 55, hard cash.
—*Sophie Tucker*

You need to plan for financial security in your old age if

- you have not accumulated, and think it unlikely you will accumulate, financial assets that generate enough income to support a comfortable lifestyle.

- you work full-time for an employer with no retirement plan.

- you work part-time and do not qualify for coverage under an employer's retirement plan.

- you might not be employed by the same employer long enough to qualify for retirement benefits.

- your family's income would be drastically reduced by the death or disability of a working husband.

- your husband's company retirement plan has no benefits for surviving spouses of active or retired workers.

- you are divorced and you can't count on your ex-husband to ante up.

- you were divorced at an age too old to find remunerative employment and too young to receive the benefits Social Security provides to ex-wives.

- you expect to receive an inheritance or you have an affluent, generous husband, but you know that nobody looks out for you as well as you do yourself.

What You Can Expect to Receive From Social Security

If you are married, you have the option of receiving retirement benefits based either on your own employment record or your husband's, whichever is higher. A wife who has not worked long enough to earn Social Security credits may receive, at age 65, half of the retirement pay her husband receives at age 65. The amount you receive is reduced if you choose to begin spousal retirement benefits at age 62.

All widows and ex-wives of covered workers may begin receiving survivor's benefits if they are 60 years old or older. You do not lose those benefits if you remarry *after the age of sixty*. Monthly payments are made to a widow of any age if she has a child under 16 or disabled.

A divorced woman qualifies for social security on her ex-husband's record if she is unmarried, 62 years old or older, and was married for at least 10 years. She may receive 50% of his benefits at 65, 37.5% at age 62.

Call your local Social Security Adminstration office for information about the dollar amount of monthly benefits you might receive when you, your husband or ex-husband retire.

What You Should Know About Your Employer's Retirement Benefits

• What kind of retirement plan is provided? A pension plan? A profit-sharing plan? A Simplified Employee Pension (SEP)? A 401(k)? A 403(b)?

• Years of employment before you are *vested* (have a nonforfeitable entitlement to retirement benefits).

• Age or years of employment to receive full retirement benefits.

• Minimum age at which you receive a pension and how much you will receive.

• The formula used to calculate the dollar amount of your pension.

• Whether or not the plan's benefits will be reduced by Social Security benefits.

• Whether or not you may make voluntary contributions to a retirement plan, and if so, how much. Are these pre-tax or after-tax contributions?

• Whether or not you have the option of receiving your retirement benefits as a lump sum distribution—all at once—rather than as a pension paid out over a period of time.

• Whether or not your spouse will collect a part of your accumulated benefits if you die before retirement.

• Whether or not you will continue to receive your husband's pension if he dies, how much and for how long.

• Whether or not a surviving spouse has the option of taking death benefits as a lump sum or in periodic installments.

• Whether or not you are entitled to the value of your pension earned to date if you can no longer work because you are permanently and totally disabled.

• Whether or not you may borrow from the plan for your children's education, a home purchase, medical expenses or other purposes.

• That contributions are unlikely to continue during a "break in service" such as a temporary layoff, maternity leave or other leave of absence.

• That if you are married you must name your spouse as the beneficiary of your retirement benefits upon your death unless he consents to the naming of someone else.

• That an ex-spouse has the right to obtain a Qualified Domestic Relations Order which permits him to share your retirement benefits and receive survivor's benefits.

• That once a year you should receive a summary of your plan's annual financial report. You also have the right to request, once in every twelve-month period, a written statement of your earned benefit and vested interest in that benefit.

Distribution Options and Tax Consequences of Employee Retirement Benefits

You may have the option of receiving your retirement benefits as a lump sum distribution—all at once—or as a pension paid out over a period of time.

Employer contributions to retirement plans and the income earned on those contributions are exempt from income taxes until withdrawals are made. The distribution received by an employee or the employee's beneficiary is taxable unless the distribution is rolled over into an Individual Retirement Account (IRA). There is no tax on contributions made by an employee with after-tax dollars.

Anyone who is 59 1/2 or older may elect special five-year income averaging on a lump-sum distribution. Income averaging can lower the tax bill on your distribution by spreading it over the current year and four previous years. If you turned 50 before January 1, 1986, you have a choice between special five-year income averagng and special ten-year income averaging which permits income spreading and, therefore, a lower tax bite, over ten years.

A surviving spouse has the option of "rolling over" the *taxable* portion of her deceased spouse's retirement benefits into a tax-deferring IRA.

If you are vested and leave a company, you may roll over the taxable portion of your distribution into an IRA and not pay taxes on the distribution, even if you go to work for another company with a retirement plan. You *may* roll over the distribution you receive from a former employer's retirement plan into a second employer's plan if the new employer is willing.

How Much Will You Need to Retire?

Provide the following information on the worksheet on page 99:
(1) Your current age.
(2) The age at which you would like to retire.
(3) Number of years until the age at which you would like to retire.
(4) How much income you would like during your retirement years. (Add new expenses you will acquire in retirement to expenses listed on the Personal Income Statement on pages 4 and 5 and deduct expenses you no longer will incur.)

(5) The current market value of *all* your currently owned *income-producing* assets. Deduct the value of your home and personal property from TOTAL ASSETS on page 9. Include your home if you plan to sell it and become a renter. Adjust income needs to account for rent payments.

Then calculate:

(6) The **pre**-tax income you will need to generate the **after**-tax income you set as your goal above. To find your tax bracket, use this formula and the current tax tables on pages 138-139:

$$\frac{\text{After-tax income}}{(1.00 - \text{Tax bracket})} = \text{Pre-tax income}$$

Example
$$\frac{\$25,000}{(1.00 - 0.28)} = \$34,700$$

(7) The income you can expect to receive each year from employer, government and other retirement plans.

(8) The amount of income you could earn on your currently owned income-producing assets. (Include IRA and Keogh assets if your retirement age is 59 1/2 or older.) Assume you will be able to earn 8% each year.

Example $50,000 (Income-producing assets)
            x 0.08
            $ 4,000

(9) Add annual income from all expected sources of retirement income in (lines 7 and 8).

(10) Deduct the amount on line 9 from the amount on line 6. The balance is the additional income needed to reach your pre-tax retirement income goal.

(11) What lump sum must be accumulated to earn the additional income? Again, assume that you could earn an average rate of return of 8%. Divide the amount on line 10 by 8%.

Example $$\frac{\$10,700}{8\%} = \$133,750$$

(12) *Inflation* Up to this point we have been working with *current* dollars and assuming that their purchasing power in the future will be the same as it is today. But what if inflation causes prices to rise an average of 5% per year between now and the time you retire?

Using the Compound Interest Table at the end of the chapter, multiply the lump sum you need to accumulate (in our example, $133,750) by the figure at the intersection of 5% and the number of years until you retire (in our example, 25 years).

$$\$133{,}750 \times 3.3864 = \$452{,}900$$

In this example, $452,900 must be accumulated in 25 years in order to generate the income that $133,750, earning 8%, could produce in current dollars.

(13) Calculate how much you will have to save each year to accumulate the additional funds needed. Use the Accumulation Table at the end of the chapter. Assume that your average annual return is 8%.

Divide the additional amount you need to accumulate by the figure at the intersection of 8% and the number of years until you retire. This is how much you need to set aside each year.

Example $$\frac{\$452{,}900}{\$\ 78{,}954} = \$5{,}700$$

If your income needs are less, if your investments earn more than 8% each year, if prices increase at a lower rate than 5% each year, if tax rates are lower, if Social Security and pension benefits are higher than currently projected, then you will need to accumulate a smaller amount each year until you retire.

If your income needs are greater, if your investments earn less than 8% each year, if prices increase at a higher rate than 5% each year, if tax rates are higher, if Social Security and pension benefits are lower than currently projected, then you will need to accumulate a larger amount each year until you retire.

HOW MUCH WILL YOU NEED TO RETIRE?

		Example
(1) Current age	_____	40
(2) Planned retirement age	_____	65
(3) Number of years until retirement	_____	25
(4) Desired after-tax annual income during retirement years	_____	$25,000
(5) Current market value of all currently owned income-producing assets	_____	$50,000
6) Pre-tax income needed to generate after-tax income in (4) above	_____	$34,700

SOURCES OF RETIREMENT INCOME:

(7) Social Security	_____	$10,000
Company Retirement Plan #1	_____	$10,000
Company Retirement Plan #2	_____	
Annuity #1	_____	
Annuity #2	_____	
Other	_____	
Other	_____	

(8) Income earned on currently owned assets	_____	$4,000
(9) ESTIMATED RETIREMENT INCOME	_____	$24,000
(10) Additional income needed to meet retirement needs	_____	$10,700
(11) Amount needed to generate $ _____ at 8%	_____	$133,750
(12) 5% inflation-adjustment to (11) above	_____	$452,900
(13) Annual savings needed each year for _____ years	_____	$5,700

Individual Retirement Accounts (IRAs)

What is an IRA? An IRA is an umbrella term for the savings accounts and investments we buy to provide for financial security in our retirement years. An IRA is not an investment itself, but rather a legal structure within which the government permits us to save for retirement.

Who may have an IRA? Anyone who has earned income, even if self-employed, only works part time, or participates in an employer's retirement plan; recipients of alimony; and homemakers whose spouses set up a "spousal" IRA.

How much may be contributed to an IRA?
Individual IRAs: 100% of earned income with a maximum of $2,000 each year.
Spousal IRAs: a maximum of $2,250 a year to two accounts, one for each spouse. The $2,250 may be divided any way the spouses choose, so long as neither account has more than $2,000.

Up to $2,000 or $2,250 is the most you may contribute to an IRA in one year, but you may contribute as little as an institution will accept. Do not be deterred from opening an IRA if you haven't got $2,000.

Tax consequences of putting money into and taking money out of an IRA You do not pay federal income taxes on funds placed in an IRA *if* neither you nor your spouse has another retirement plan *or* if one of you participates in another retirement plan but you file a joint income tax return and have an adjusted gross income (AGI) of no more than $40,000. The limit for single taxpayers is $25,000.

Your annual contributions are partially deductible if you participate in another retirement plan but you are single and have an AGI between $25,000 and $35,000 or you are married and have an AGI between $40,000 and $50,000. If your AGI exceeds $35,000 or $50,000 (whichever is applicable), no part of your contribution is deductible, but you are permitted to make non-deductible contributions to an IRA.

Taxes on income earned by the investments in *all* IRAs are deferred until withdrawals of income are made. This permits your IRA to grow faster than if the income were not tax-sheltered.

Simplified Example

	IRA	*Nonsheltered investment*
Investment income earned—Year 1	$100	$100
Income available for reinvestment—Year 2 (Assume 28% tax bracket)	$100	$72

You may begin to make withdrawals from an IRA when you are 59 1/2 years old. You must begin to withdraw from the account when you are 70 1/2 years old. If withdrawals are made before you are 59 1/2, there is a 10% excise-tax penalty, plus regular income tax due on the amount withdrawn, unless you are totally disabled.

You have two distribution options for getting money out of your IRA: installment payouts and a lump-sum distribution (all at one time). All distributions from IRAs are taxed at ordinary income rates. Distributions paid in periodic installments from an IRA are taxed during the year payments are made. The remaining funds are not taxed until they are withdrawn. (The non-deductible IRA contributions you make with *after*-tax dollars will not be taxed at all.) Deductible contributions and reinvested income withdrawn at one time as a lump-sum distribution are taxed during the year of the distribution. You may use regular five-year income averaging in this case.

Everyone who has earned income, alimony or an employed husband should have an IRA whether or not the annual contribution is "deductible." It imposes the discipline of regular saving and, if done every year until you are 60 or 70 years old, exemplifies the old saying that "out of little acorns, big oaks grow."

How, where and when to open an IRA Commercial banks, savings institutions, insurance companies, brokerage firms, mutual funds and trust companies act as *trustees* for IRAs. They maintain records of your annual contributions and account earnings, and invest or re-invest at your direction.

An IRA may be invested in a wide range of assets: savings certificates, money-market accounts, stocks, bonds, mutual funds, annuities, tax shelters, and certain gold coins issued by the U.S. mint. Tax shelters and coins are relatively risky investments for anyone depending on her IRA for retirement income. The best IRA investments earn income *or* offer the prospect of long-term growth potential or both.

At some institutions, you are able to buy only the company's own investments for IRAs, such as savings certificates or annuities. Mutual-fund organizations which permit shifting in and out of different kinds of "growth" and "income" funds offer greater investment diversity, but you are still restricted to a particular set of funds. *Self-directed IRAs*, available through some banks, brokerage firms and mutual-fund sponsors, provide the most variety and flexibility. You are charged an annual management fee as well as commissions on security transactions in your account, but you may direct the account manager to buy and sell among a wide choice of allowable IRA investments.

You are permitted to make an IRA contribution every year that you have earned income, receive alimony or qualify for a spousal IRA. You may add to previous IRA investments *or* choose a different IRA manager each year *or* choose a different IRA investment with the same manager each year.

You do not have to make one year's contribution to the same IRA account as the previous year's. You do not have to keep a previous year's IRA indefinitely. You may move an IRA account from one institutional trustee to another as often as you wish.

If you have an IRA distributed to yourself, the reinvestment must be made within 60 days of closing the old account. This sort of change may be made only once a year.

IRAs may be opened after January 1 during the year for which a contribution is being made and as late as April 15 of the next year.

Keogh Plans

Who may have a Keogh plan?
- Self-employed individuals.
- Partnerships.
- "Moonlighters" covered by employer retirement plans.
- Employees of an employer who has a Keogh plan must be included if they work full-time and meet minimum age and term-of-employment qualifications.

How much may be contributed to a Keogh plan? Beginning in 1987, the following options are available to self-employed individuals who have Keogh Plans:

- A maximum contribution of *10%* of *net income* to a *Money Purchase Pension Plan*, or a *Defined Benefit Pension Plan* which provides for contributions greater than 10% and is actuarily computed to provide a pension of as much as $90,000 a year.

- A maximum contribution of *15%* of *net income* to a *Profit-sharing Plan.*

- A maximum of $30,000 per year on *total* contributions to a Money Purchase Pension Plan and Profit-sharing Plan.

Anyone who has income from "moonlighting" or her own business should take advantage of the opportunity to shelter retirement savings from taxation. Consult a retirement planning specialist to determine whether a "money purchase plan," a "defined benefits plan," or a "profit-sharing plan"—all of which can be organized under the Keogh umbrella—is best for you.

How, where and when to open a Keogh plan Keogh plans may be opened with the same financial service organizations that offer IRAs. Individuals or organizations with large plans ($100,000 or more) might consider using an investment advisor.

Unlike IRAs, Keogh Plans must be *opened* by December 31. Like IRAs, the investment need not be made until the following April 15.

Tax consequences of putting money into and taking money out of a Keogh plan Taxes are payable on deductible contributions and income earned by investments in a Keogh Plan when withdrawn. Potentially taxable funds remaining in the account are not taxed until they are withdrawn. Contributions that were nondeductible when made are never taxed because they were made with after-tax dollars.

Proprietors and partners may begin to make withdrawals from a Keogh Plan at 59 1/2 years old, and *must* begin to withdraw from the account at 70 1/2 years old. If withdrawals are made prior to age 59 1/2, there is a 10% income tax penalty plus regular income tax due on the amount withdrawn. On the other hand, employees may make withdrawals without penalty before age 59 1/2 if they retire or terminate their employment.

There are no penalties for withdrawals of voluntary contributions made with after-tax dollars by either employers or employees.

If an employer or employee becomes totally disabled, her total share may be withdrawn without penalty at any time.

Distribution options of Keogh plans *Lump sum* withdrawals of total contributions and reinvested income may be made at one time, or *installment payouts* may be made for a specific period of time (e.g., 20 years); for the plan participant's lifetime; or over the life of the participant and spouse.

Salary Reduction Plans

Salary reduction plans, also known as 401(k)s for the section of the Internal Revenue Code authorizing them, are set up by employers for their employees. Each salaried worker is permitted to make an annual contribution of up to $7,000 to the firm's 401(k). A company may make matching contributions to its employees' accounts, sometimes as much as $1 for every $2 the employee provides. As with deductible IRAs, neither annual contributions nor reinvested income is taxed until withdrawn from the account. If a participant experiences "financial hardship" at a pre-retirement age and wishes to draw down her 401(k) account, she will pay a 10% penalty tax on the distribution.

401(k)s are highly recommended as a tax-sheltered retirement vehicle for those with take-home pay that exceeds current needs.

Simplified Employee Pension Plans

A Simplifed Employee Pension (SEP) is an Individual Retirement Account (IRA) set up by an employer for each employee and funded by the employer. Each employee designates where she wants her IRA opened (e.g., First National Bank, The Best Mutual Fund Company) and how she wants her money invested (e.g., a six-month savings certificate, The Best High Income Fund). The employer may make a tax-deductible contribution of as much as 15% with a $30,000 maximum to each employee's SEP-IRA. Like 401(k) participants, employees may make annual salary reduction contributions for as much as $7,000. Compared with other retirement plans, SEPs are simple to set up and administer.

A SEP-IRA may be your best bet if you are on your own or have a small company. Check with a retirement benefits specialist.

IRA Rollovers

The key letter in IRA rollover is "I" for individual. This is a tax-sheltered retirement account that serves as a repository for lump-sum distributions received by retired workers, by employees who have left their place of employment, by employees whose company retirement plan has been terminated, or by spouses whose deceased spouse participated in a company retirement plan.

The recipient of a lump-sum distribution is not *required* to roll over such funds into an IRA, but if she doesn't, she must pay income tax when she receives them. Therefore, rollovers are for those who do not anticipate a near-term need and want to maximize pre-tax earnings on their investments.

It is possible to make a partial rollover. For example, if Charlotte receives $10,000 from her ex-employer's profit-sharing plan, she can keep out $2,500 for herself and put $7,500 into an IRA rollover with a mutual fund. She will then be liable for taxes on the $2,500.

The amount of the lump-sum distribution that goes into the account is the *only* money the account will ever receive, other than income on the investment. The same conditions for investing, withdrawing and paying taxes that apply to other IRAs also apply to IRA rollovers.

Annuities

An annuity is an investment purchased from a life-insurance company that guarantees an income for a specific period of time. Annuities frequently are purchased to provide retirement income. For example, an employer or worker makes monthly contributions to an annuity during working years; then a monthly check is paid from the annuity to the employee (the annuitant) during the post-working years.

An annuity can be a good retirement investment for a homemaker who has no income of her own but wants to plan for financial security in her old age. An annuity can be purchased with one lump sum (a single-premium annuity) or built up over time like a savings account.

Annuities purchased with pre-tax dollars are like IRAs purchased with deductible contributions. Taxes on contributions and reinvested income are not paid until the annuitant begins to take money out of the annuity. Sometimes purchased through salary *reduction* plans.

Annuities purchased with after-tax dollars defer taxes on the *reinvested income* until paid out to the annuitant. Taxes are not due on contributions, of course; the tax has already been paid. Sometimes purchased through salary*deduction* plans.

Fixed-premium annuities require that the same contribution be made at fixed intervals throughout the pre-retirement period (e.g., $100 a month, $1,000 a year).

Variable-premium annuities allow participants the option of making different contributions each year (e.g., $1,000 one year, $1,500 the next).

Single-premium annuities are often purchased with lump-sum proceeds received by the beneficiary of a life-insurance policy or by a retired worker. Income payments may begin immediately, in which case they are taxable; if income is reinvested and deferred, the tax is also deferred.

Fixed-payment annuities guarantee that a specific income will be paid periodically for a specific number of years or throughout an annuitant's lifetime. *The guaranteed rate when you begin to take income out might be higher than the guaranteed rate in subsequent years.*

Variable-payment annuities guarantee income payments for a specific number of years or throughout an annuitant's lifetime. The amount of each payment varies according to the income earned by the investments, usually common stocks, in the annuity's portfolio. Variable-payment annuities offer the possibility of a higher income than fixed-payment annuities, but also less stability and dependability.

Combined fixed-payment and variable-payment annuities offer an annuitant the opportunity to receive part of her annuity from a fixed-payment investment and part from a variable-payment investment. The annuitant decides the proportion of her retirement income she will receive from each investment. Generally, no changes can be made in these proportions once the annuitant begins taking income out of the annuity.

How Much May Be Contributed to an Annuity?

Annuities purchased for IRAs, Keogh plans and other qualified retirement plans are subject to the same annual limitations as other investments purchased for these accounts.

Employees of public school systems and other nonprofit organizations may make an annual tax-deductible contribution to an annuity of up to $9,500 of their salaries. Employer contributions are limited to 20% of an employee's taxable income. There is no limit on employee contributions made with after-tax dollars.

Each insurance company's policy determines the *minimum* contribution it will accept.

Annuity Payment Options

Single-life annuity payments stop with the annuitant's death.

Single-life annuity with a guaranteed payment period pays annuity income for the remainder of a "guaranteed payment period" to an annuitant's beneficiaries if she dies during the guaranteed period of 10, 15 or 20 years. If she lives longer than the guaranteed period, she receives her annuity for life but no payments are made to her beneficiaries.

Joint and survivor annuity is an annuity for two or more persons. The amount of the monthly payment may be the same or less after the death of one of the annuitants. *Joint annuity payments are less than single-life annuity payments.*

How Much Will It Cost to Buy or Sell an Annuity?

The amount of money actually invested in an annuity on your behalf by a brokerage firm or insurance company may be less than the amount of your contribution if there is a sales charge, or front load, on each premium.

Example

Annual premium	$1,000
8% sales charge	- 80
Amount invested	$ 920

Charges for management fees and other expenses might also be deducted from your premiums.

If you decide to terminate your annuity or take a partial cash withdrawal, a termination charge might be deducted from the proceeds, calculated as a percentage of the proceeds or as a flat rate.

Take these various charges into account when you compare an annuity's tax advantages with non-tax-sheltered investments. Remember, the interest earned on an annuity accumulates tax free until you take it out.

ACCUMULATION TABLE

Rate of Interest	5 years	10 years	15 years	20 years	25 years	30 years	35 years	40 years
5.0%	5,802	13,207	22,657	34,719	50,113	69,761	94,836	126,840
5.5%	5,889	13,584	23,641	36,786	53,966	76,419	105,765	144,119
6.0%	5,975	13,972	24,673	38,993	58,156	83,802	118,121	164,048
6.5%	6,064	14,372	25,754	41,349	62,715	91,989	132,097	187,048
7.0%	6,153	14,784	26,888	43,865	67,676	101,073	147,913	213,610
7.5%	6,244	15,208	28,077	46,553	73,076	111,154	165,820	244,301
8.0%	6,336	15,645	29,324	49,423	78,954	122,346	186,102	279,781
8.5%	6,429	16,096	30,632	52,489	85,355	134,773	209,081	320,816
9.0%	6,523	16,560	32,003	55,765	92,324	148,575	235,125	368,292
9.5%	6,619	17,039	33,442	59,264	99,914	163,908	264,649	423,239
10.0%	6,716	17,531	34,950	63,002	108,182	180,943	298,127	486,852
11.0%	6,913	18,561	38,190	71,265	126,999	220,913	379,164	645,827
12.0%	7,115	19,655	41,753	80,699	149,334	270,293	483,463	859,142
13.5%	7,323	20,814	45,672	91,470	175,850	331,315	617,749	1,145,486
14.0%	7,536	22,045	49,980	103,768	207,333	406,737	790,673	1,529,909
15.0%	7,754	23,349	54,717	117,810	244,712	499,957	1,013,346	2,045,954
20.0%	8,930	31,150	86,442	224,026	566,377	1,418,258	3,538,009	8,812,629

Dollar amounts indicate accumulation at end of specific time periods of $1,000 invested each year at different compound rates of interest.

Example: $1,000 invested at 8% each year for 10 years would be worth $15,645 at the end of that time period. $1,500 invested at 8% each year for 10 years would be worth $23,468.

COMPOUND INTEREST TABLE

Years	5%	6%	7%	8%	9%	10%	11%
1	1.0500	1.0600	1.0700	1.0800	1.0900	1.1000	1.1100
2	1.1025	1.1236	1.1449	1.1664	1.1881	1.2100	1.2321
3	1.1576	1.1910	1.2250	1.2597	1.2950	1.3310	1.3676
4	1.2155	1.2625	1.3108	1.3605	1.4116	1.4641	1.5181
5	1.2763	1.3382	1.4026	1.4693	1.5386	1.6105	1.6851
6	1.3401	1.4185	1.5007	1.5869	1.6771	1.7716	1.8704
7	1.4071	1.5036	1.6058	1.7138	1.8280	1.9487	2.0762
8	1.4775	1.5938	1.7182	1.8509	1.9926	2.1436	2.3045
9	1.5513	1.6895	1.8385	1.9990	2.1719	2.3579	2.5580
10	1.6289	1.7908	1.9672	2.1589	2.3674	2.5937	2.8394
11	1.7103	1.8983	2.1049	2.3316	2.5804	2.8531	3.1518
12	1.7959	2.0122	2.2522	2.5182	2.8127	3.1384	3.4985
13	1.8856	2.1329	2.4098	2.7196	3.0658	3.4523	3.8833
14	1.9799	2.2609	2.5785	2.9372	3.3417	3.7975	4.3104
15	2.0789	2.3966	2.7590	3.1722	3.6425	4.1772	4.7846
16	2.1829	2.5404	2.9522	3.4259	3.9703	4.5950	5.3109
17	2.2920	2.6928	3.1588	3.7000	4.3276	5.0545	5.8951
18	2.4066	2.8543	3.3799	3.9960	4.7171	5.5599	6.5436
19	2.5270	3.0256	3.6165	4.3157	5.1417	6.1159	7.2633
20	2.6533	3.2071	3.8697	4.6610	5.6044	6.7275	8.0623
21	2.7860	3.3996	4.1406	5.0338	6.1088	7.4002	8.9492
22	2.9253	3.6035	4.4304	5.4365	6.6586	8.1403	9.9336
23	3.0715	3.8197	4.7405	5.8715	7.2579	8.9543	11.0263
24	3.2251	4.0489	5.0724	6.3412	7.9111	9.8497	12.2392
25	3.3864	4.2919	5.4274	6.8485	8.6231	10.8347	13.5855
26	3.5557	4.5494	5.8074	7.3964	9.3992	11.9182	15.0799
27	3.7335	4.8223	6.2139	7.9881	10.2451	13.1100	16.7386
28	3.9201	5.1117	6.6488	8.6271	11.1671	14.4210	18.5799
29	4.1161	5.4184	7.1143	9.3173	12.1722	15.8631	20.6237
30	4.3219	5.7435	7.6123	10.0627	13.2677	17.4494	22.8923
31	4.5380	6.0881	8.1451	10.8677	14.4618	19.1943	25.4104
32	4.7649	6.4534	8.7153	11.7371	15.7633	21.1138	28.2056
33	5.0032	6.8406	9.3253	12.6760	17.1820	23.2252	31.3082
34	5.2533	7.2510	9.9781	13.6901	18.7284	25.5477	34.7521
35	5.5160	7.6861	10.6766	14.7853	20.4140	28.1024	38.5749
36	5.7918	8.1473	11.4239	15.9682	22.2512	30.9127	42.8181
37	6.0814	8.6361	12.2236	17.2456	24.2538	34.0039	47.5281
38	6.3855	9.1543	13.0793	18.6253	26.4367	37.4043	52.7562
39	6.7048	9.7035	13.9948	20.1153	28.8160	41.1448	58.5593
40	7.0400	10.2857	14.9745	21.7245	31.4094	45.2593	65.0009

COMPOUND INTEREST TABLE

Years	12%	13%	14%	15%	16%	17%	18%
1	1.1200	1.1300	1.1400	1.1500	1.1600	1.1700	1.1800
2	1.2544	1.2769	1.2996	1.3225	1.3456	1.3689	1.3924
3	1.4049	1.4429	1.4815	1.5209	1.5609	1.6016	1.6430
4	1.5735	1.6305	1.6890	1.7490	1.8106	1.8739	1.9388
5	1.7623	1.8424	1.9254	2.0114	2.1003	2.1924	2.2878
6	1.9738	2.0820	2.1950	2.3131	2.4364	2.5652	2.6996
7	2.2107	2.3526	2.5023	2.6600	2.8262	3.0012	3.1855
8	2.4760	2.6584	2.8526	3.0590	3.2784	3.5115	3.7589
9	2.7731	3.0040	3.2519	3.5179	3.8030	4.1084	4.4355
10	3.1058	3.3946	3.7072	4.0456	4.4114	4.8068	5.2338
11	3.4785	3.8359	4.2262	4.6524	5.1173	5.6240	6.1759
12	3.8960	4.3345	4.8179	5.3503	5.9360	6.5801	7.2876
13	4.3635	4.8980	5.4924	6.1528	6.8858	7.6987	8.5994
14	4.8871	5.5348	6.2613	7.0757	7.9875	9.0075	10.1472
15	5.4736	6.2543	7.1379	8.1371	9.2655	10.5387	11.9737
16	6.1304	7.0673	8.1372	9.3576	10.7480	12.3303	14.1290
17	6.8660	7.9861	9.2765	10.7613	12.4677	14.4265	16.6722
18	7.6900	9.0243	10.5752	12.3755	14.4625	16.8790	19.6733
19	8.6128	10.1974	12.0557	14.2318	16.7765	19.7484	23.2144
20	9.6463	11.5231	13.7435	16.3665	19.4608	23.1056	27.3930
21	10.8038	13.0211	15.6676	18.8215	22.5745	27.0336	32.3238
22	12.1003	14.7138	17.8610	21.6447	26.1864	31.6293	38.1421
23	13.5523	16.6266	20.3616	24.8915	30.3762	37.0062	45.0076
24	15.1786	18.7881	23.2122	28.6252	35.2364	43.2973	53.1090
25	17.0001	21.2305	26.4619	32.9190	40.8742	50.6578	62.6686
26	19.0401	23.9905	30.1666	37.8568	47.4141	59.2697	73.9490
27	21.3249	27.1093	34.3899	43.5353	55.0004	69.3455	87.2598
28	23.8839	30.6335	39.2045	50.0656	63.8004	81.1342	102.9666
29	26.7499	34.6158	44.6931	57.5755	74.0085	94.9271	121.5005
30	29.9599	39.1159	50.9502	66.2118	85.8499	111.0647	143.3706
31	33.5551	44.2010	58.0832	76.1435	99.5859	129.9456	169.1774
32	37.5817	49.9471	66.2148	87.5651	115.5196	152.0364	199.6293
33	42.0915	56.4402	75.4849	100.6998	134.0027	177.8826	235.5625
34	47.1425	63.7774	86.0528	115.8048	155.4432	208.1226	277.9638
35	52.7996	72.0685	98.1002	133.1755	180.3141	243.5035	327.9973
36	59.1356	81.4374	111.8342	153.1519	209.1643	284.8991	387.0368
37	66.2318	92.0243	127.4910	176.1246	242.6306	333.3319	456.7034
38	74.1797	103.9874	145.3397	202.5433	281.4515	389.9983	538.9100
39	83.0812	117.5058	165.6873	232.9248	326.4838	456.2980	635.9139
40	93.0510	132.7816	188.8835	267.8635	378.7212	533.8687	750.3783

13 Estate Planning: Who Gets What After You're Gone

"Estate planning" refers to decisions we make now regarding the transfer of possessions and the payment of taxes at the end of our lifetime. The primary vehicles used to implement these decisions are *lifetime gifts, trusts and wills*.

Why Everyone Should Have a Will

Anyone who has assets with monetary or sentimental value should have a will. If you die without a will (intestate), your assets are distributed by the *state and not necessarily to whom you would want*.

> Like many people, Alan never got around to writing a will. He assumed that his wife Lynn would inherit his possessions whether he had a will or not. In fact, when Alan died, the intestacy law of the state of Pennsylvania directed that Lynn receive only $30,000 plus one-half of the balance of his $100,000 estate. The remaining $35,000 was inherited by their children. Because they were under 18 years of age, a guardian was appointed by the court to look after the children's share. Lynn had to consult with the guardian about every expense for the children from her daughter's piano lessons to her son's orthodontist.
>
> Also, since he hadn't written a will, Alan hadn't named an *executor*, the person responsible for disbursing a deceased person's assets. Therefore, the court had to select an *administrator* for Alan's estate. During the time it took for the administrator to be appointed and a bond for the adminstrator to be posted, Alan's assets were "frozen" and unavailable to his family for their use.

Joint ownership of property is not a satisfactory substitute for a will. It doesn't name a guardian for your young children if you and your husband die in an accident. It doesn't provide for the piano you want to leave to a favorite niece or the annuity for an elderly parent. It also doesn't protect your children's inheritance if your husband remarries and leaves everything to his second wife.

If you don't have a will, or if your old will needs updating, make an appointment with a lawyer as soon as possible. Because you pay for a lawyer's time, go to your meeting prepared with the following information:

• A list of your assets.

• Whom you want to inherit your assets.

• What you want each beneficiary to receive.

• How your business or professional practice should be disposed of.

• The timing of asset transfers: i.e, immediately, over a period of time, at one specific time in the future.

• Whether assets should be distributed directly to the beneficiaries or held in trust.

• Your first choice(s) as executor(s).

• Your second choice(s) if your first choice(s) can't or won't serve.

• Your first and second choices as trustee, if needed (Trustees often are, but need not be, the same persons as executors).

• Guardians of minor children (who will look after their personal well-being).

What Are The Duties of An Executor?

The executor's job is to gather together the decedent's assets, pay the estate's debts and taxes, and distribute bequests to the decedent's heirs. *Specifically*, the executor is responsible for some or all of the following:

• Locating the decedent's will.

• Filing the will for probate. This is the official procedure by which an executor is appointed and the will is verified as the decedent's last will.

- Locating and making an inventory of all the decedent's assets, including the contents of her safe deposit box.

- Listing all the decedent's debts and verifying the validity of claims presented for payment.

- Selecting an attorney as counsel for the estate if needed and if the decedent had not done so. Executors should request that counsel charge for services on a hourly fee basis, *not as a percentage of the estate's value*, that a written estimate of counsel's fee be given when counsel is selected, and that counsel's billing time be accounted for when the final bill is presented.

- Acquiring copies of the death certificate to be used as confirmation of the decedent's death for banks, insurance companies, Social Security claims, etc.

- Filing claims and collecting life-insurance proceeds payable to the estate or beneficiaries.

- Closing the decedent's bank and brokerage accounts and opening a checking account for the estate.

- Investing income earned by the estate's assets in a short-term interest-earning account such as a money-market fund.

- Maintaining records of all income earned by the estate's assets before the assets are distributed to the beneficiaries.

- Determining the value of all assets on the day of the decedent's death and on the day exactly six months after the decedent's death. The latter is known as the "alternate valuation date" and may be used by the executor to pay a lower federal estate tax if the total value of assets is lower than it was on the date of death.

- Arranging for appraisals of real estate and personal belongings.

- Selling assets to raise funds to pay off debts and taxes.

- Collecting debts owed to the decedent.

- Notifying beneficiaries of their bequests.

- Determining the appropriate time to make distributions to beneficiaries.

- Arranging for the preparation of federal and state death-tax returns and income-tax returns, usually by a lawyer or accountant who specializes in estate planning.

- Paying the federal estate tax, which comes due within nine months of a decedent's death, and paying state death taxes, if any, when due.

- Paying federal and state income taxes on income earned by the estate.

- Arranging for the preparation of a final accounting for the appropriate authorities after all bequests are distributed and debts and taxes are paid.

Who to Name as Executor

First Choice A family member or close friend who is your age or younger, knowledgable enough about financial, tax and legal matters to carry out some of the duties of executor herself, and capable of selecting competent professionals for the services she cannot provide.

Second Choice As co-executors, a family member whom you can trust to look after the personal well-being of other family members and an experienced professional (your lawyer or accountant) or a bank trust department.

Executor Fees

Relatives and close friends who serve as executors are entitled to, and may take, a fee from your estate. Professionals and institutions always charge a fee. Customarily, the fee is a percentage of the estate's assets and a percentage of income earned on investments, although a lawyer or accountant may be willing to bill on an hourly fee basis.

Estate, Gift and Inheritance Taxes

Federal estate taxes are levied on estates with a value of $600,000 or more *after* administrative expenses, burial expenses, and charitable bequests are deducted. *There are no federal estate taxes on bequests to a spouse.*

Federal gift taxes are due on any gift of more than $10,000 made each year to some one other than your husband. The gift tax usually is paid by the person making the gift (the donor). *There are no federal gift taxes on gifts between spouses.*

State estate taxes are imposed by some states. The federal estate tax is reduced by the amount of the state estate tax.

State gift taxes are imposed by some states. The amount of the gift tax may vary according to the recipient's relationship to the donor.

State inheritance taxes are imposed by some states on bequests made to beneficiaries. Life-insurance proceeds and assets owned jointly by husband and wife might be exempt. The amount of the tax may vary according to the closeness of the beneficiary's relationship to the decedent. Inheritance taxes usually are paid by the estate.

There are no income taxes on received gifts or inheritances.

Annual Tax-Free Gifts

The federal government permits each individual to give to an unlimited number of other individuals as much as $10,000 a year for as many years as the donor wishes without these gifts being subject to the federal gift tax.

In 1987 Barbara gave $10,000 each to her two daughters, $5,000 to a granddaughter, and $5,000 to a retiring employee on his 65th birthday. She plans to give another $10,000 to each daughter and $5,000 to her granddaughter in 1988. Barbara pays no gift tax on these gifts because none is more than $10,000.

The annual exclusion is doubled to $20,000 for married couples, even if only one spouse has income or assets, so long as the other spouse consents to the gift.

Tax-free gifts are not the same as the charitable contributions for which you receive a *tax deduction* on your income tax return.

The Use of Trusts in Estate Planning

A *trust* is a legal arrangement under which one individual (the "grantor," "creator" or "settlor" of the trust) transfers ownership of some or all of her assets to a *trustee* (another individual or an institution) who manages the assets for the benefit of the trust's *beneficiaries*. A trust can be put into effect during the creator's lifetime (an *"inter vivos"* trust) or after her death (a "testamentary" trust).

An *inter vivos* trust (also referred to as a "living trust") may be *revocable*. It may be terminated or changed during the settlor's lifetime. After the settlor's death, the trust becomes irrevocable. It then is adminstered for the benefit of beneficiaries according to the terms of the trust instrument (deed of trust). Assets in a revocable trust are considered part of a decedent's estate and are subject to federal estate taxes, as they can be taken back by the settlor at any time.

If the trust is *irrevocable*—the settlor gives up the right to change or terminate the trust—and if the settlor does not receive income from the trust, the assets are not part of her taxable estate. They *are* taxed as a gift at the time assets are transferred to the trust.

Trusts are set up to control the disposition and use of assets and/or to minimize death taxes.

How Trusts Work

Trust creator: Jane, 45 years old, married. Purpose of trust: To assure that Jane's children inherit from Jane's estate if she dies before her husband.

Jane has $100,000 in stocks and bonds. She names her irrevocable trust as the beneficiary in her will. A deed of trust—the document that explains the terms of a trust—says that Jane wishes her husband Robert to receive all the income from the trust during his lifetime. When he dies, Jane's trustees are directed to distribute the money in equal shares to their three children.

Robert also has $100,000 in stocks and bonds. If Robert remarries and decides to leave his $100,000 to his second wife, Jane's children are assured of inheriting at least the $100,000 their mother left in trust.

Trust creator: Ella, mother of two adult sons. Purpose of trust: To provide for a severely handicapped son without jeopardizing his eligibility for public benefits.

Ella has named her trust as owner of a $100,000 life-insurance policy. It is a "sprinkle" trust—the trustees are instructed to distribute, or sprinkle, principal and/or income according to each son's need. The deed of trust tells her trustees that they should not pay for services which her disabled son could receive from the government, such as vocational training and health care. Ella's granddaughter will receive the trust's assets after her uncle dies so that the trust cannot become part of his estate.

"Sprinkle" trusts also may be used by parents who do not want to support a habit or association of which they disapprove but who are reluctant to disinherit a child who might some day mend her ways.

What Assets Will The Trust Receive?

Any asset which is owned by the trust's creator—cash, stocks, bonds, real estate, etc.—may be signed over to trustees. A trust also may be the beneficiary of a life-insurance policy or retirement benefits. *Assets that are owned jointly cannot be left to a trust. They pass automatically to a surviving spouse even if he or she is the beneficiary of the trust.*

Whom to Name as Trustee

As with estate executors, individuals and institutions named as trustees should be selected because they are experienced, competent and trustworthy. Not everyone is fortunate enough to have a relative or friend or professional advisor who fits the bill.

One of the reasons for naming a bank trust department as trustee is that it specializes in the organization and adminstration of trusts and estates. Trust departments employ investment managers, investment analysts, trust administrators, fiduciary law specialists and tax specialists who efforts are coordinated for the benefit of the trustee's clients. An individual trustee might die or become incapacitated, but a corporate trustee is immune to the vagaries of human mortality. And although the best trust administrators are sensitive to the needs and wishes of their clients, they remain unbiased and independent from the entreaties and rivalries of family members.

Also, an institutional trustee is likely to have larger financial resources than an individual trustee, and therefore be in a better position to make restitution in cases of fraud or mismanagement.

Most banks or trust companies will serve as "co-trustee" with a relative and/or valued personal adviser of the trust's creator. If you are reluctant to appoint a corporate trustee for a trust that becomes effective after your death, you can stipulate in the trust agreement that the individual trustee has the right to remove the corporate trustee and name another in its place. Or, you might set up an *inter vivos* revocable trust which provides you with the opportunity to judge the trustee's competency during your lifetime.

Where Things Are

After the trauma of losing a loved one, the task of tracking down the location of a will, bank accounts, insurance policies, etc., can be an emotionally draining and often frustrating experience for family members.

List the location of all documents and evidence of ownership of assets that might be needed by your family members and estate executors. Keep a copy of this list in a bedside or desk drawer. Let someone know it exists.

	LOCATION	ACCOUNT NO.
Will	_____	_____
Life Insurance policies	_____	_____
	_____	_____
	_____	_____
Bank Accounts	_____	_____
(include ID numbers	_____	_____
for automatic teller machines)	_____	_____
Credit Cards	_____	_____
	_____	_____
	_____	_____
Brokerage Account	_____	_____
Security certificates	_____	_____
Real estate deeds	_____	_____
Rental leases	_____	_____
Unpaid bills	_____	_____
Notes on outstanding loans	_____	_____
Notes receivable	_____	_____
Automobile titles	_____	_____
Other _____	_____	_____
_____	_____	_____
Safe-deposit boxes	_____	_____
Safe-deposit box keys	_____	_____

14 Who Owns What: His, Hers and Ours

The question of how an asset should be owned—soley or jointly, and if solely, by whom—arises for couples in two important aspects of financial decision-making: who has the right to use, sell or give away an asset; and the *tax* advantages or disadvantages associated with sole or joint ownership.

The Different Kinds of Legal Ownership

Sole ownership One person owns the property and may give it or sell it to whomever he or she wants.

Tenancy by the entirety A form of joint ownership between spouses. Each has an interest in the entire property. Neither spouse may dispose of the jointly owned asset without the other's consent. At the death of one spouse, the asset automatically becomes the property of the surviving spouse.

Joint ownership with rights of survivorship Also referred to as a joint tenancy. Each owner or "tenant" owns a half-interest in the property, which may be sold or given to a third party while the original owners are living. At the death of one owner, the asset automatically becomes the property of the surviving owner.

Tenancy in common Each owner or tenant owns a half interest in the property, which may be sold or given to a third party during the lifetimes of the joint owners. A tenancy in common differs from a joint tenancy in that when a joint owner dies, his or her share passes to his or her heirs.

Community property Eight states—Arizona, California, Idaho, Louisiana, Nevada, New Mexico, Texas and Washington—are known as "community property" states. All income and assets acquired while living as a married couple in a community property state are owned 50-50. Assets which are inherited, received as gifts, acquired before the marriage, or acquired in a noncommunity property state are considered separate property. Each spouse may bequeath his or her share of the community property to whomever he or she wishes; there are no rights of survivorship with community property.

Why Every Married Woman Should Have Assets in Her Own Name

On page 26 we discussed why a married woman should establish her own financial identity: to be prepared for the possibility of divorce or widowhood, to learn by doing, to have the satisfaction of being in control of her own financial well-being. Having assets of her own is not only a way for a woman to establish her own financial identity; it also can be crucial to her financial *security*.

The advantages of having assets in one's name alone become apparent—and necessary—when a marriage breaks up. A woman dependent on her husband for most or all of her financial support has no guarantee of financial security if assets are held in joint name or the assets are in his name alone. She is totally dependent on his good will to liquidate joint assets that will provide her with the means to support herself. Frequently, she must hire a lawyer and engage in protracted, expensive litigation until she receives her rightful share of the joint assets.

And, sadly, we hear too often of older women with poor prospects for training or employment who are left by their husbands and do not receive the income they would have shared had they remained married.

Even happily married women should have assets of their own so that they can share them with whomever they wish during their lifetimes and leave them to whomever they wish when they die. There is no assurance that even the most devoted husband will look after his wife's mother or any other people his wife cares about after she's gone.

This is not to say that *all* assets a couple owns jointly must be divided 50-50. It is convenient for both spouses to have access to a joint checking account. It saves time, and possibly money, for jointly owned assets to become automatically and immediately the possessions of a surviving spouse. And some assets, such as a house, are neither practically nor easily divisible.

But there are other assets, such as savings instruments, securities, investment real-estate properties and cars, that can be owned solely by either spouse. For example, if a couple purchases 200 shares of common stock, 100 shares can be registered in each name alone as easily as registering 200 shares in joint name.

Prenuptial Agreements

It has been said that the first time around you have bridesmaids and ushers; the second time, bankers and lawyers. Any woman entering into a second marriage, no matter how modest her means, and especially if there are children from the first marriage, should have an prenuptial agreement with her new spouse.

A prenuptial agreement is a legal contract written before a marriage takes place. The agreement usually is prepared by a lawyer. It describes the financial arrangements agreed to by the prospective spouses while they are married and the distribution of assets after their death or divorce.

The agreement provides the legal clarification of who owns what and to whom it goes in case of death or divorce. But a prenuptial agreement also can eliminate resentment and misunderstandings between spouses and among parents and children by dealing with a delicate situation realistically and fairly.

In some states, a husband or wife has the legal right to a specific share of a deceased spouse's estate if less than that share of the decedent's property is left through a will to the surviving spouse. To eliminate the possibility of such a claim, a prenuptial agreement may include a clause in which one or both spouses gives up the right to *elect against the will*, that is, claim their legal share of an estate.

A prenuptial agreement does not prevent spouses from sharing their assets with one another or including one another in their wills. Its purpose is to strengthen each spouse's position before they marry with respect to the disposition of his or her assets.

Divorce and Separation Agreements

These are the legal documents, usually negotiated by lawyers, that stipulate who gets what when a marriage breaks up. Although the ultimate division of a couple's assets is determined by many factors—including a lawyer's negotiating skills—the property settlement laws in the state in which they reside carry a heavy weight.

Assets categorized as "community property" are parceled out 50-50 in the eight so-called "community property" states. To some degree, *equitable distribution* guidelines are followed in the remaining 42 states. Specific divvying-up criteria vary from state to state, but the prevailing principle of equitable distribution is that all assets aquired during a marriage, no matter how they were owned during the marriage (except perhaps gifts and inheritances) can end up in a "his" column, "her" column or a "to-be-sold-and-proceeds-split" column.

Two important concepts introduced by equitable distribution laws are the recognition of the homemaker's contribution to her family's financial well-being, and the inclusion of a working spouse's retirement benefits in the aggregated marital property. In accordance with the Domestic Relations Tax Reform Act of 1984, an ex-spouse receives a share of the working spouse's retirement benefits and survivor's benefits unless she specifically gives up her rights to these benefits in writing.

Living Together Agreements

Living together is like being married in many ways, but it always differs from a marriage in one important respect: when the relationship breaks up or one of the partners dies, there are minimal social, governmental and legal guidelines to protect or determine property rights.

The best way to avoid the prospect of a nasty court battle or being dependent on a loved one's good intentions is to have a Living Together Agreement (LTA). It is particularly important for couples who purchase a residence together to agree in advance on such issues as whether to own the property jointly if only one partner has provided the down payment but the other shares mortgage payments, whether to own the property jointly if only one partner has resources for the down payment and mortgage payments, and how or whether the house will be sold and the proceeds divided if they split up or one of them dies.

As with writing a will, it's a good idea for a couple to consult a lawyer. Before a meeting is arranged, you should put down on paper the issues to be dealt with in your LTA and how you would like to have them resolved.

Income and Estate Taxes

When a two-income married couple files a joint income-tax return, they often pay a higher tax than unmarried counterparts. Check with your accountant to see whether your tax bill could be lower if you and your husband divide assets and pay taxes as a married couple filing separately.

No federal estate tax is paid when assets are given by one spouse to the other during their lifetime or through a will. However, an affluent husband often has more assets in his name alone, such as his business or professional practice, a retirement plan and securities, than his wife has.

Consult a lawyer who specializes in estate planning about the feasibility of divding assets and setting up trusts so that total taxes paid by your heirs on your estates are minimized.

15 The Tax Man Cometh

No financial decision should be made solely on the basis of tax considerations, but every legitimate opportunity to eliminate, minimize or defer taxes should be explored.

Tax planning means thinking ahead. Tax planning should not be saved for tax preparation season. It should be done all year every year. It should be a part of the overall and continuous financial planning we discuss in the next and final chapter of the workbook.

Keeping Up With Changes in The Tax Laws

Income tax rules and regulations seem to change as often as the seasons. In many cases, the new laws affect financial decisions that must be made before the end of a calendar year. Major tax reforms, such as the 1986 Tax Act, are front-page news in most newspapers, and are covered extensively by specialized financial publications. When you see an item that seems to affect you, call your accountant or the local Internal Revenue Service (IRS) office for clarification.

Also, buy an income tax guide, such as Sylvia Porter's *Income Tax Guide,* the J. K. Lasser *Tax Institute Guide,* the Prentice-Hall *Federal Tax Handbook,* or get a free copy of "Your Federal Income Tax for Individuals" from the IRS. These publications explain current federal tax return forms line by line.

Consult Experts

Meet with your accountant several times a year to discuss your needs and objectives. Don't expect to do deliberative tax planning on April 1 when you and the accountant are under pressure to meet the deadline for filing that year's return by April 15.

Not all accountants are equally competent as tax advisers. If your accountant's ability is limited to converting tax records into tax returns once a year and you feel a need for more professional assistance, find another accountant. The fee you pay for good tax planning, like the fee for tax-return preparation, may be a tax-deductible expense. It can be more than offset by the money you get to keep in your pocket and out of Uncle Sam's.

Keep Good Records

Have a ledger to record all sources of personal income and expenditures (if you have a business, keep separate records).

Keep all receipts for purchases and payments with tax consequences in a file, divided topically (e.g., Medicine and Drugs; Charitable Contributions; Moving Expenses). Make complete notations in your checkbook for all deposits and payments.

	Date	Deposits	
General Motors Dividend	10/14	$60.00	Oct 15 1987 Order of *B.B. Kimmelman D.D.S.* *For Elizabeth* **Tax deductible dental expense* *$25.00*

At the beginning of the year, label a large manila envelope, "Taxes 19__." Use it for storing W-2 forms, "1099s" (confirmations of dividends and interest paid by banks, mutual funds and corporations), tax returns, the IRS instruction manual and any other tax-related materials that arrive in the mail.

Who Must File a Tax Return?

• Anyone claimed as a dependent on someone else's tax return whose gross income is more than $500.

• Single taxpayers whose gross income is more than $4,400 in 1987 (changes to $4,950 in 1988).

• A "head of household" whose gross income is more than $4,440 in 1987 ($6,350 in 1988).

• Married couples whose gross income is more than $7,560 in 1987 ($8,900 in 1988).

These amounts are higher for taxpayers over 65 years of age or blind.

Which Tax Form Should You Use?

Form 1040 A, known as the "short form." Should be used if your income is less than $50,000, your income comes from earned income, interest or dividends, and you have no adjustments to income or itemized deductions other than an Individual Retirement Account.

Form 1040 EZ, the "easy" form. May be used by single taxpayers with no dependents, taxable income of less than $50,000, no dividend income and interest income of no more than $400.

Form 1040, for all other taxpayers who have taxable income greater than $50,000 from various sources, who itemize deductions and have adjustments to income and credits to report.

How to Calculate Your Taxable Income on Form 1040

Take out your most recent tax return. Go through it line by line to see if there are additional savings you can make for the next year, taking into account tax law changes that will apply to your 1987 and subsequent returns. All line references are to 1986 Form 1040. Page references are to this workbook.

Filing status (lines 1 through 5) Most of the time, tax rates are lower for married couples who file joint returns than for married couples who file separately, women who file as head of household rather than as single or married filing separately, and widows who file as qualifying widows rather than as single or head of household. If you are uncertain which category is better for you, calculate your taxes both ways.

Exemptions (Lines 6a-6f) You reduce your taxable income by claiming as exemptions yourself, your spouse, your children and elderly parents for whom you provide substantial support. You may *not* take an exemption for anyone who takes an exemption for himself or herself on another tax return.

On line 36, you may deduct from your Adjusted Gross Income $1,900 in 1987, $1,950 in 1988 and $2,000 in 1989 for each exemption claimed on Line 6f. After 1987, the benefit of the personal exemption for high taxable incomes will be phased out.

The double exemption previously allowed for the blind and those over 65 years old has been eliminated. Since January 1, 1987 the blind or elderly who do not itemize deductions receive a standard deduction "bonus" of $750 if single and $600 if married ($1,500 and $1,200 if both over 65 and blind).

Income (Lines 7-23) All *personal service income* earned as wages, salaries, tips, commissions, fees and some employee benefits are taxable.

All *dividend income* is taxable.

Interest earned on bank accounts, money market funds, savings certificates, U.S. Treasury issues and corporate bonds is taxable. *Interest on most but not all municipal bonds is* not *taxable* (page 53). Tax-exempt interest must be reported on all returns filed for tax years beginning in 1987.

Refunds of state or local income taxes claimed as deductions on federal tax returns in previous years are considered taxable income in the year you receive the refund.

Alimony is taxable income for the recipient and a tax reduction item for the payor. (Child support payments are neither taxable nor tax deductible.)

Business income or loss If you have your own business, you may take deductions for such expenses as telephone service, office supplies, postage, advertising, travel costs, business publications and contributions to pension funds and profit-sharing plans. If your home is your principal place of business, you may deduct a part of the operating and maintenance costs, but no more than the amount of gross income earned from your business.

Capital gains and losses A *capital gain* is the increase in value of a real or financial asset. A *capital loss* is a decrease in value, the opposite of a capital gain. If you paid $200 for a painting in 1985 and sold it this year for $400, your capital gain is $200. If you sold 100 shares of stock for $3,000 for which you paid $5,000, you've got a $2,000 capital loss.

Taxes must be paid on capital gains, but only when an appreciated asset is sold. At that time, you have a *realized* gain. If appreciated assets are not sold, you have an *unrealized* or "paper" gain.

Before 1987, a gain on assets owned less than six months was taxed as ordinary income. Of gains on assets owned six months or longer, only 40% was taxed, and the maximum tax was 20%. Beginning in 1988, all gains, no matter how long the asset was owned, will be taxed at the same rate as all other income. In 1987, the "transition year" from the old tax law to the new, the tax on a short-term gain (on an asset owned less than six months) may be as high as 38.5% and the tax on a long-term gain (an asset owned at least six months) may be as high as 28%.

Two exceptions to the above:
(1) If you sell your house for more than you paid for it, you do not have to pay a capital gains tax if, within two years, you use the sales proceeds to buy a new residence.

(2) If you are 55 years old or older, sell a house you have lived in for at least three of the past five years, and do not buy a new house, you may take a tax-free capital gain of up to $125,000. Married couples are considered to be one taxpayer for this exemption. Only one spouse need be 55 years old to qualify.

Just as the value of an asset can rise, it can fall. If it does, you have a *capital loss*. The only good thing we can say about a capital loss is that it can be used to lower taxes. Up to $3,000 of capital losses may be subtracted from capital gains or other taxable income earned in the same year the loss is incurred. Losses greater than $3,000 may be "carried forward" and used in future years to offset capital gains and other taxable income.

Distributions from pensions, IRAs and annuities funded by an employer or by your tax-deductible contributions and interest are taxable in the year received. Distributions from retirement plans funded with after-tax dollars are not taxable.

Rental income If you manage your own real estate and have an Adjusted Gross Income (Line 32) of less than $100,000, you may use losses up to $25,000 to offset non-rental income. The loss deduction is phased out for AGIs over $100,000.

Limited partnerships After 1990, limited partners in tax shelters, including real estate shelters, will not be permitted to use losses generated by the shelters (primarily depreciation and interest payments) to offset salary and investment income. Losses will be deductible only as an offset to an equal amount of income from other limited partnerships. During the transition period, 65% of excess losses will be deductible in 1987, 40% in 1988, 20% in 1989 and 10% in 1990. The phase-out applies only to tax shelters purchased before January 1, 1987.

Social Security benefits are taxable if the sum of Adjusted Gross Income, 50% of Social Security income and tax-free interest income exceeds $25,000 for a single taxpayer or $32,000 for married taxpayers.

Adjustments to Income (Lines 24-31) *Moving expenses* are deductible only for taxpayers who itemize their deductions rather than take the standard deduction on Line 34.

Employee business expenses are now considered part of *miscellaneous deductions* (Schedule A Lines 20-23). If you paid for such work-related expenses as educational programs, uniforms, union dues, subscriptions to trade publications, meals and transportation away from home *and* you were not reimbursed by your employer, you may deduct these expenses only if you itemize *and* they are part of miscellaneous expenses which exceed 2% of your Adjusted Gross Income.

Employees who are "outside saleswomen": Try to arrange to have your employer reimburse you for all your expenses.

IRAs Since 1986, contributions to Individual Retirement Accounts are deductible only for individuals with no company retirement plan or those in plans whose Adjusted Gross Incomes do not exceed $25,000 ($40,000 if married and filing joint returns). All others with earned income may make annual IRA contributions with after-tax dollars. Taxes on IRA investment *income* will continue to be deferred for everyone until funds are withdrawn.

Self-employed individuals may contribute as much as 25% of their earned income to their *Keogh plans,* with a maximum annual contribution of $30,000.

Alimony is a deductible expense for the payor.

Spousal earnings deduction The provision allowing the lesser of 10% or $3,000 of a lower-earning spouse's income to be deducted from gross income is no longer in effect.

Income - Adjustments to Income = Adjusted Gross Income (line 32)

Adjusted Gross Income
- [Standard Deduction + Exemption Allowances] = Taxable Income

Standard Deduction In 1987, the standard deduction is $1,880 for married taxpayers filing separately, $2,540 for single taxpayers and heads of households, and $$3,760 for married couples filing jointly.

These amounts increase in 1988 to $2,500 for married taxpayers filing separately, $3,000 for single taxpayers, $4,400 for heads of households and $5,000 for married couples filing jointly.

Exception: Blind or elderly taxpayers receive a standard deduction "bonus" of $750 if single and $600 if married or head of household ($1,500 and $1,200 if both over 65 and blind). The 1988 standard deduction schedule becomes effective for the blind and elderly in 1987.

Exception: The maximum standard deduction for a taxpayer with unearned income but no earned income who is claimed as a dependent on another tax return is $500.

Itemized Deductions—Schedule A We are able to further reduce our taxable income by listing, or itemizing, personal and work-related expenses on Schedule A of Form 1040 if deductible expenses exceed the amounts permitted under the standard deduction.

Medical and dental expenses that exceed 7.5% of Adjusted Gross Income are deductible. You may deduct the cost of office visits to psychologists, chiropractors, acupuncturists, and Christian Science practitioners, transportation to and from medical treatment, and special equipment or home renovations made for the convenience and safety of a handicapped person, as well as expenses for traditional health care services, medication and health insurance premiums.

Taxes you paid State and local income taxes, real-estate taxes and personal property taxes are deductible. State and local sales taxes are no longer a deductible expense.

Interest you paid Mortgage interest on first and second homes is fully deductible for loan amounts that do not exceed the original cost of a property plus improvements. A loan larger than that amount is fully deductible only if used for educational or medical purposes.

The deductibility of interest on student loans, car loans, credit-card balances, department-store charge-account balances, life-insurance policy loans and other consumer interest payments will be phased out over five years beginning with the 1987 tax year. You may deduct 65% of your personal interest payments in 1987, 40% in 1988, 20% in 1989, 10% in 1990 and 0% in 1991.

Interest deductions on funds borrowed to finance investments are limited to the amount of investment income earned by the taxpayer.

Charitable contributions you made are deductible only if you itemize.

Uninsured casualty and theft losses that exceed 10% of Adjusted Gross Income plus $100 are deductible.

Miscellaneous deductions Since January 1, 1987, such expenses as tuition, employment-agency fees, work clothes and uniforms, union and professional dues, tax return preparation fees, dues to trade associations, safe deposit box rentals and the purchase of this workbook are deductible, but only for that part of the total that exceeds 2% of your adjusted gross income.

Calculate your Taxable Income (line 37)

Tax rate schedules In 1987, the fifteen brackets that ranged from 11% to 50% were reduced to two brackets of 15% and 28%. A portion of the taxable income of high-income earners will have a 5% surcharge, making the highest marginal rate 33% (See Tax Tables on Pages 138-139). For 1987 only, there will be five brackets, from 11% to 38.5%, blending old and new tax rates.

Alternative minimum tax The alternative minimum tax, intended to recoup tax revenues from high-income earners who pay little or no tax, has been raised from 20% to 21%. If you have tax shelters, exercise stock options or purchase certain "private activity" municipal bonds, you may be liable for a tax hike via the AMT.

Income averaging 1986 was the last year for which a taxpayer was able to lower her tax bill by "spreading" income over the current year and four previous years.

Unearned income of children under fourteen Since December 31, 1986, all unearned income of $1,000 or more in the name of a child under age fourteen is taxed at his or her parents' marginal (highest) tax rate.

Taxable Income – Credits = Tax Payment

Credits are dollar-for-dollar reductions of taxes due (line 40).

Credit for child and dependent care expenses can be taken by working parents or full-time students for caretaking expenses for all children under age fifteen and for disabled dependents of any age. Taxpayers with adjusted gross incomes less than $10,000 may receive the maximum credit of $720 for one dependent and $1,440 for two or more dependents. The credit decreases as income increases, levelling off at $480 for one dependent and $960 for two or more at an AGI of $28,000.

Credit for the elderly or permanently and totally disabled can be taken if you are age 65 or older, or under 65 with a permanent and total disability. The amount of the credit cannot be more than the amount of federal taxes you would owe without the credit. The credit is generally available only to individuals and couples whose incomes place them on a level at which Social Security benefits are not taxable.

The earned income credit is available to you if your adjusted gross income is less than $11,000 *and* you have a child who is less than nineteen years old, a full time student, or disabled. The maximum credit is $550 for qualified taxpayers with AGIs of no more than $6,500. The credit decreases as income increases.

Estimating the Coming Year's Taxes

If your income arrives in irregular amounts, or from sources not subject to an employer's withholding, you must file an estimated quarterly tax return every three months with the Internal Revenue Service. If your state has an income tax, you also must file with the state.

The estimate is based on your expectation of the amount of income you will receive and when you will receive it. If you underestimate and pay less than 90% of the taxes you wind up owing by the end of the year, you will be charged a penalty for underwithholding—unless the taxes paid are at least equal to the previous year's tax payments, even if the current year's income and tax obligation turn out to be higher.

You are not required to pay estimated taxes if you expect
• your unearned income (interest, dividends, rent, etc.) to be less than $500.
• your earned income to be less than $20,000 and you are unmarried, a head of household, a surviving spouse, or married to a nonworking spouse.
• your earned income to be less than $10,000 between you and your employed spouse.
• your tax payment to be less than $500.

Estimated quarterly tax payments are due on the 15th of April, June, September and January. Form 1040-ES for filing estimated payments may be obtained from the IRS.

Will Your Tax Return Be Audited?

An *audit* is a review of your tax return by an agent employed by the Internal Revenue Service. According to *All You Need to Know About the IRS,* by Paul Strassels and Robert Wool, the purpose of tax audits is *to keep taxpayers honest through the fear of being caught doing something dishonest.*

Every tax return received by the IRS is keyed into an IRS computer. A number of taxpayers in each income bracket is selected at random by the computer for audit. Other returns send up a "red flag" to the computer when a figure is out of line for "average" or "normal" deductions in the taxpayer's income bracket, occupational category or geographic area.

About one per cent of all tax returns filed by individuals are audited each year. The odds of being audited increase as your income increases. Some taxpayers are never audited. Some are frequently audited.

Audits can be made up to six years following the year in which a return is filed. Generally, only returns for the immediate past three years are audited. However, all cancelled checks, bank statements and other tax records should be kept for at least six years. There is no time limit on the IRS's right to audit fraudulent returns.*

---

*There may be non-tax reasons for looking up information on old tax returns, so the probable answer to how long to keep them and other financial records is: for as long as you have the storage space. If you want to replace a lost or discarded tax return, file Form 4506 (Request of Copy of Tax Form) with your local IRS service center.

An audit can begin and end with a brief review of your return by an IRS agent at his desk, never involving you, or it can consist of close scrutiny and require your participation.

What to Do if You Are Called for an Audit

You will receive written notification of the time and date of an interview with an IRS agent and a request for information relating to specific items on your tax return.

• If you have reported all *taxable* income and *legitimate* deductions, you have nothing to fear from an audit.

• You may go to the audit alone or with your spouse. Your accountant or lawyer may accompany you or go in your place as your authorized representative.

• You decide whether to hold the audit at the IRS office, your home, your office or your accountant's or lawyer's office.

• Be prepared to justify with written documentation the items in question. This might include the worksheets you used to prepare your tax return, bank statements and cancelled checks, bank deposit slips, confirmations of dividends and interest, confirmations of security purchases and sales, expense account records, your business appointment calendar, receipts for cash expenses, and receipts for cash or nonmonetary charitable contributions.

• Answer questions politely and precisely. Do not volunteer information for which you are not asked.

• If the auditor concludes that you have underpaid (e.g., the agent disallows a contribution of old clothes to the Salvation Army or some business entertainment expenses you've deducted), and you or your accountant believe the deductions are justified, you may ask to speak with the auditor's supervisor. If this brings no satisfaction, you may appeal the auditor's decision to the IRS Appellate Division and, after that, to federal Tax Court.

TAX TABLES

1987

Single Taxpayers

If taxable income is more than	but not more than	Tax rate is	of amount over
0	$1,800	11%	$0
$1,800	16,800	$198 + 15%	1,800
16,800	27,000	2,448 + 28%	16,800
27,000	54,000	5,304 + 35%	27,000
54,000		14,754 + 38.5%	54,000

Married Couples

If taxable income is more than	but not more than	Tax rate is	of amount over
0	$3,000	11%	$0
$3,000	28,000	$330 + 15%	3,000
28,000	45,000	4,080 + 28%	28,000
45,000	90,000	8,840 + 35%	45,000
90,000		24,590 + 38.5%	90,000

Heads of Households

If taxable income is more than	but not more than	Tax rate is	of amount over
0	$2,500	11%	$0
$2,500	23,000	$275 + 15%	3,000
23,000	38,000	3,350 + 28%	28,000
38,000	80,000	7,550 + 35%	45,000
80,000		25,250 + 38.5%	90,000

TAX TABLES

After 1987

Single Taxpayers

If taxable income is more than	but not more than	Tax rate is	of amount over
0	$17,800	15%	$0
$17,850	43,150	$2,678 + 28%	17,850
43,150	89,560	9,762 + 33%	43,150
89,560		28% of entire amount	

Married Couples

If taxable income is more than	but not more than	Tax rate is	of amount over
0	$29,750	15%	$0
$29,750	71,190	$4,463 + 28%	29,750
71,190	149,250	16,265 + 33%	71,190
149,250		28% of entire amount	

Heads of Households

If taxable income is more than	but not more than	Tax rate is	of amount over
0	$23,900	15%	$0
$23,900	61,650	$3,585 + 28%	29,750
61,650	123,790	14,155 + 33%	61,650
123,790		28% of entire amount	

16 Nobody Looks Out for You as Well as You Do: Financial Planning in Action

Financial planning is the most effective way to organize your financial life. It provides a structure within which you can think ahead, set goals, and coordinate the financial decisions that will help you reach those goals.

You began the financial planning process in Chapter 1 by Getting Organized and Setting Goals. Now you should be ready to move on to Step Three, Developing a Financial Plan, and Step Four, Implementing Your Plan.

STEP 3
DEVELOPING A FINANCIAL PLAN

On page 11 you listed your financial goals, the aspirations that motivate you to work hard, save and invest. Perhaps you said you want to open the candy store you yearned for as a little girl. Perhaps you want to have enough money to escape northern winters and bask in California sunshine. At this stage we get to the nitty-gritty of how you turn those visons of bonbons and palm trees into reality. Now is the time to figure out *how much* you will need and *when* you will need it. Your projections ultimately will be affected by future income, the rate of inflation and the rate of return on your investments, but you will be operating within the framework of a carefully considered, coordinated plan.

Begin by filling in a copy of the worksheet on the next page for each goal you set for yourself on page 11 except retirement planning. Use the worksheet on page 99 for retirement planning.

We provide for long-term goals only after we've set aside our savings nest egg (Chapter 2) and provided for adequate insurance (Chapter 4).

How Much Must You Save and Invest Each Year?

(1) Describe your goal _____
(Buying a house, daughter's college tuition, etc.)

(2) How much money will you need _____
to reach your goal? (Use additional lines _____
for financial goals with staggered time _____
horizons, such as the four years you _____
will pay college tuition.)

(3) When will you need the money
to reach your goal? _____ years

(4) How much have you set aside
to reach this goal? _____

(5) Additional amount to be
accumulated _____

Turn to Accumulation Table (page 109)

6. Find the *column* that corresponds to the rate
of interest you think you could earn each year
during the accumulation period. Enter the rate
of interest here. _____ %

7. Divide the additional amount you need
to accumulate by the figure at the *intersection* of
the above rate of interest and above number
of years. Multiply by $1,000. Enter here. $ _____

This is how much you need to set aside *each
year* to accumulate the lump sum on line 5.

How Much Must You Set Aside Each Year?

Total the amounts on Line 7 on each worksheet and on the last line of page 99 for retirement planning. Because different goals have different time horizons, you will need to accumulate more during some years than others.

Year	Goal	Year	Goal
1.	_____	16.	_____
2.	_____	17.	_____
3.	_____	18.	_____
4.	_____	19.	_____
5.	_____	20.	_____
6.	_____	21.	_____
7.	_____	22.	_____
8.	_____	23.	_____
9.	_____	24.	_____
10.	_____	25.	_____
11.	_____	26.	_____
12.	_____	27.	_____
13.	_____	28.	_____
14.	_____	29.	_____
15.	_____	30.	_____

Where Will The Money Come From?

The money to reach your long-term goals comes primarily from three sources: surplus income (what's left over after paying for personal and household expenses), currently owned assets, and inheritances. Do you think your surplus income, currently owned assets, and inheritances will provide the funds you need to reach your goals?

If not, what can you do to increase your income? Cut back on expenses? Are you willing to take on additional risk to increase the income you earn on your investments? Can you modify your financial goals—aim only for the most wanted results, stretch out accumulation periods—so that your goals are realistic and attainable?

STEP 4
IMPLEMENTING YOUR FINANCIAL PLAN

This is the stage at which you select the savings instruments, insurance coverage and investments that make your financial plan a reality. This is when you decide whether you want to invest in stocks, bonds or real estate to reach your retirement goal. Do you want to keep your savings nest egg in a money market fund or savings certificate? Does whole life or term insurance provide the best coverage for your family?

Where Do You Go For Help?

At some point you'll seek professional assistance for information, for advice, or for following through on the different aspects of your plan. The chart on page 145 is a general directory of the different financial institutions and individuals who offer the financial products and services you will want to consider.

How To Choose A Financial Advisor

Throughout this workbook, we have stressed the importance of being well-informed and having control over your financial life. But there is a limit to what even the best-informed and most efficient woman can do for herself. This is why there are professional advisers, individuals who have the experience and expertise to point out the different options and the facilities to implement financial decisions.

Ideally, a financial adviser is able to assist in all aspects of a client's financial affairs. There is a small but growing group of professionals called financial planners who take this coordinated approach. Most financial professionals continue to specialize—in investments, accounting, law, insurance, etc.—and serve their clients within their areas of expertise.

How do you find a competent financial adviser? The best way is through a personal referral. Ask for recommendations from someone whose opinion you value. If that is not possible, pick several names with addresses convenient to your home or office from the telephone directory. (This potluck method is as likely to produce satisfactory results as calling the office of a national professional association such as the American Bar Association.)

You should not make a commitment to hand over your financial affairs to anyone until you sit down for awhile and get to know one another. When you meet you should ask about professional credentials and experience, how much the service will cost, and for the names of several clients you may call for a reference. This is the time to decide whether you will feel comfortable working with the people you've met. Do you like them? Do they inspire confidence? Seem to know what they're talking about? Make recommendations suitable for your particular situation and needs? Act as if you will be a valued customer?

Unfortunately for people of modest means, the services of a good financial adviser do not come cheaply.* Most work for an hourly fee rate. Some advisers scale their fees according to the client's income. Others set a minimum fee, such as $1,000 or $2,000. However, because the fees for financial advisory services are considered "expenses associated with the production or collection of income," they may be tax deductible.

You want to choose a financial adviser who works on a fee-paying basis rather than on commission, because this is the best way to assure that the advice you are getting is objective advice. There are, for example, people calling themselves "financial planners" who sell a product, such as mutual funds or insurance. They tell prospective clients there is no charge for their advisory services, but too often the clients find that the best way to reach their goals is to buy the products the so-called planner sells and on which he or she earns a commission. It is not impossible, but it is more difficult, to provide an objective analysis when your motivation is to sell something.

Whomever you choose, remember that it's *your* money and *your* well-being that's at stake. Do not continue to patronize an individual or organization if you're not getting the quality of service you think you should receive. Don't be intimidated by the presence of a "busy, self-important expert." Don't be afraid to ask "dumb" questions or say, "That doesn't sound quite right to me." Don't move on to a new topic until you feel confident you understand the subject being discussed.

We need and should use professionals for their experience and ability to implement our financial decisions, but remember: *Nobody looks out for your interests as well as you do.*

*To rectify this situation, a group of female financial professionals in Philadelphia have organized a financial clinic called The Women's Financial Center. We provide workshops and personal consultations at nominal rates for women who could not otherwise afford such services.

Where to Go for Help

FINANCIAL INSTITUTIONS OR INDIVIDUALS

FINANCIAL PRODUCT or SERVICE	Bank	Thrifts	Money Market Fund	Insurance Agent	Stock and Bond Broker	Mutual Fund Manager	Real Estate Broker	Silver and Gold Dealer
Savings Instruments	X	X	X					
Insurance				X				
Stocks, Bonds and Mutual Funds					X	X		
Real Estate							X	
Silver and Gold	X							X
Collectibles								
Tax Shelters					X			
Retirement Planning	X	X		X	X	X		
Estate Planning				X				

Where to Go for Help

FINANCIAL INSTITUTIONS OR INDIVIDUALS

FINANCIAL PRODUCT or SERVICE	Investment Adviser	Bank Trust Department	Collectibles Vendor	Lawyer	Accountant	Tax Lawyer	Financial Planner
Savings Instruments							X
Insurance							X
Stocks, Bonds and Mutual Funds	X	X					X
Real Estate							X
Silver and Gold	X						X
Collectibles	X		X				X
Tax Shelters	X			X	X	X	X
Retirement Planning	X	X					X
Estate Planning		X		X	X		X
Tax Planning					X	X	X

FINANCIAL PLANNING IN ACTION

STEP 5
PERIODICALLY REVIEW
AND REVISE YOUR PLAN

A financial plan is like a road map. It helps you get to where you think you want to go. But after you've set up your plan, you might decide the road you chose originally is too narrow or bumpy. Perhaps you want to take a different route.

That's why step five of the planning process is important. You want to review your plan at least once a year, and revise it if the plan no longer meets your needs or measures up to your expectations.

You'll want to make changes as your personal situation changes. There might be more or less income than you'd anticipated. The dependent children you had might have left home, or you might be closer to retirement age.

The savings instruments, investment or insurance policies you've chosen might not measure up to the expectations you had when you selected them. Cut your losses. Find another investment or another adviser, whatever you need to get back on track.

Things happen in our economy which affect your outlook and planning. A major change in the tax laws, such as the Tax Reform Act of 1986, or a string of years with double-digit inflation, can affect the financial decisions you make now and will make in the future.

Financial planning is a lifelong process, and once you begin to plan, it becomes a way of life. But the planning process must never be thought of as an end in itself. *The sole purpose of planning is to provide for the financial security and well-being of ourselves and our families.*

Are you ready to begin?
Good luck!